This book is for YOU

- Work in any kind of business-to-business sales.

- Have ever felt the frustration of not getting your calls put through.

- Have been told 'No, we don't take cold calls' by a pit-bull receptionist.

- Have been told 'No, we have a no-name policy' by a pit-bull receptionist.

- Have been told 'Can you send some information in to our info@email address' by a pit-bull receptionist.

- Believe in the power of word-of-mouth marketing, referrals and introductions.

- Like doing business by getting to know people and building relationships with them.

- Like the challenge of making cold calls but want to be better. In fact, you want to be the best!

- Understand that the more you learn, the more successful you will be.

- Are a consultant, coach, accountant, advisor, lawyer or need to look for any kind of new business.

If you're still reading, CONGRATULATIONS! You've taken the first step towards the forefront of a new era in sales. And you'll reap massive benefits as a result. So keep reading...

What salespeople like you think

"There's an old saying 'If only I knew then what I know now'. When you get the insights into how you can make LinkedIn work for you in 3 easy steps that saying rings in your ears. Most people have no idea of the potential of LinkedIn, so what's going to be easier? Carry on using those old-fashioned prospecting techniques and battling it out every day with gate keepers and lose precious time or adopt the techniques in this book and win more leads the smart way."
– **Chris Williams**, managing director, The CTI Group

"By following the steps tom explained, I've already go high-quality leads worth £60,000 to £70,000 for new contracts. All that came from implementing just a few of the tips Tom explained."
– **Hana Smiddy**, then sales and marketing manager, Goldcrest Cleaning, Warwick

"Tom has a deep understanding of Linkedin and its potential for generating future sales leads. I would highly recommend Tom to anyone that needs to grow his business."
– **Vasilis Karamalegos**, then EMEA programme manager, Procter & Gamble

"At Rivo we deal with large global clients. Making contact with the right people in very large multinational organisations is crucial. Tom's training was perfect to help us do this. A fantastic and informative session that I would highly recommend to other software sales teams."
– **Irfan Mamoojee**, global pre-sales director, Rivo Software, Warwick

"Tom was absolutely brilliant. Using the wording advised by Tom, I quickly made contact with a prospect and as a direct result of that meeting now have regular work. I wholeheartedly recommend Tom's LinkedIn training. It really does generate more business and it did for me."
– **Joan Goodger**, food safety trainer

"Initially I was not sure what I would learn from the training, as I had used LinkedIn for a little while. However, I was amazed by the amount that I did not know about LinkedIn and how much Tom taught me. I would highly recommend the LinkedIn training - very impressed!"
– **Emma Candlin**, JHPS Ltd, Staffordshire

"Tom's social media and LinkedIn training is well worth attending. I am now really well equipped to build my network of contacts on LinkedIn and ultimately connect with potential clients. I would not hesitate to recommend Tom's course and I am really looking forward to his follow up event."
– Julie Mrowicki-Green, business psychologist, Purple Tulip

"I can highly recommend Tom for his LinkedIn training course which I have just attended. I learned many new tips including the need to be manage my contacts and groups and make them work better for me. I am hoping to raise my profile within the legal and mediation profession by following what I learned and would highly recommend Tom's course to other legal professionals."
– Celia Christie, family dispute resolution expert, Positive Family Mediation

"I recently attended an afternoon-long Linkedin training course run by Tom, and found it very helpful. Tom offers straight forward, easy to implement advice for making Linkedin a useful and productive business tool, and presents it in a clear and concise manner that makes it seem like common sense."
– Hazel Normandale, Ant Hire, Leeds

"Tom's workshop was a great introduction to the new world of social selling and how it will help me develop business opportunities for Jigsaw CCS. We specialise in the fulfilment and delivery of creative direct mail marketing campaigns and as Business Development Manager for the company the more I can learn about other marketing channels the better. Tom's workshop was packed with great ideas, hints and tips, not just on LinkedIn but on marketing and business development in general. His training is ideal for anyone in marketing or business development who is not getting leads from LinkedIn at the moment and wants to start! Good stuff Tom!"
– Audrey Spriggs, business development manager, Jigsaw CCS

"As someone new to LinkedIn, Tom's guidance and support has helped me take that first step - which is always the hardest. He is knowledgeable and has a friendly and approachable style. The take away guide and post training-day telephone support is particularly useful in overcoming the 'knowing-doing gap' of learning anything new."
– Carole Thomson, HR consultant, Warwickshire

"Tom delivered a great training session on LinkedIn and I came away with some key concepts that will aid the growth of my business."
– David Wilson, multi-level-marketing specialist, AdvertAnywhere

"Set a bigger challenge than you are trying to master and you will overcome the original difficulty."

– *William Bennett*

About you

If you're in business, you'll know what a fantastic but sometimes frustrating profession sales can be, with rejection on the phones and the hunt for leads a constant battle.

Well, not anymore. In this book, you'll learn the EXACT process to get more leads from Linkedin in 3 easy steps.

That means more in-bound leads, more warm phone calls and more business opportunities.

Sales is, was and always will be a people business. Which is why social media is such a great way for you to build rapport with the people you want to do business with.

And, at the same time, avoid those nerve-wracking, frustrating and unproductive cold calls.

I absolutely LOVE working with other proactive B2B salespeople to help them get results more easily and more often.

My lightbulb moment

After finishing business school, my dream was to work for myself and become master of my own destiny.

My sister and I started to run manufacturing sales agency business Fibrecore.

I didn't know anyone in the manufacturing industry and, unfortunately, no-one in the manufacturing industry knew me.

After long months of rejection on the phones being blocked by gatekeepers at ever major manufacturing company the length of the UK, I was considering giving up.

Which is when I met a fellow salesman at an exhibition in Paris who mentioned how he'd got some leads for machinery sales from Linkedin.

Within a few weeks of targeted Linkedin use, I had an invitation to be a keynote speaker in front of 32 of our biggest potential customers at a conference in Germany AND appointments with companies that had rejected my cold calls.

That's when I realised the huge potential that effective use of Linkedin offered. And I decided to develop and share those ideas I first learned in Paris.

Right here and now

The result is what you're reading right now! Today, I run face-to-face and remote training courses and speak on B2B social selling, particularly Linkedin.

I think Linkedin and social media is ESSENTIAL to anyone who's serious about B2B sales today.

But I don't think it should be time-consuming or feel like a chore.

If you go to www.tommallens.com/moreleadsfromlinkedin you'll get a free report showing you 37 tried and tested ways to win more leads from Linkedin more easily and more often than ever.

Every Sales Professional needs to

Get Past the
GATEKEEPER

and straight to the
DECISION MAKER

Strategies to transform your sales success

TOM MALLENS

Published by
Filament Publishing Ltd
16 Croydon Road
Waddon, Croydon
Surrey CR0 4PA
United Kingdom
www.filamentpublishing.com
info@filamentpublishing.com
+44 (0)20 8668 2598

Printed by IngramSpark

ISBN 978-1-910125-41-0

#GetPastTheGatekeeper

Contents

It's always great to hear about new people reading this book. Drop me a line on Linkedin or Twitter (@TomMallens) anytime and let me know if or how I can help.

ARE YOU IN SALES?

Do you get frustrated when your calls aren't put through to key decision-makers?

Or do you wish more clients would come to you – instead of you chasing them?

If so, you can get 37 tried and tested ways to win more business-to-business sales leads in my exclusive free report.

Tips 5, 12 and 29 will help most salespeople ditch awkward cold calls AND get more in-bound leads more quickly and easily than ever.

They're the same tips that landed sales and marketing manager Hana Smiddy £60,000 of new business opportunities within days.

So don't miss out, download your copy now at:

www.tommallens.com/moreleadsfromlinkedin

The chance to turbo-charge your results

WIN A CHANCE OF A MYSTERY PRIZE!

If you take a pic of yourself with your copy of
Get Past The Gatekeeper and mention me on Linkedin or Twitter,
then each month, you'll be entered into a prize draw to win a
cool mystery prize.

So get snapping those selfies now!

www.linkedin.com/in/TomMallens
@TomMallens #GetPastTheGatekeeper

n case you were in any doubt, this is a book about how you can get more leads from Linkedin in 3 easy steps.

More fundamentally, it's a book about the importance of building relationships in a business-to-business (B2B) sales environment.

And how social media can help you build them quickly, easily and super-effectively.

Over the course of this book, you'll get LOADS of ideas, information and actions that you can put into practice to start getting more in-bound leads, more warm phone calls and more business opportunities.

I'll try to keep the techno-babble and marketing-speak to a minimum and focus on practical things you can do NOW to start getting results.

And also to avoid the BIG mistakes that most people unknowingly make which mean their social media efforts are more useless than a chocolate teapot.

Most importantly, I hope to dispel the ridiculous idea that social media is some kind of separate side-activity to real business.

I want to slap my palm firmly into my face every time someone says: "I don't have time for social media".

And even more so if it's followed by the dreaded: "I prefer to do business face-to-face."

Not because I think these people aren't genuinely busy. Everyone is.

And not because I think social media is a replacement for face-to-face meetings or face-to-face networking. It isn't.

But because in almost every case I've experienced, the person uttering those words – "I don't have time for social media" – is missing the point.

You see, there's a lot of nonsense talked about social media: It doesn't work; It's impossible to measure; It's a waste of time; You're too busy to do it . . . the list goes on.

But before we delve into why I believe effective use of Linkedin is a MUST-HAVE tool for anyone in B2B sales, it's time for the obligatory bit about me.

We'll come back to the much more interesting subject of you as soon as it's over. I promise!

I'm just your ordinary guy who left a decent job as editor of a national B2B trade magazine to pursue a dream of working for myself.

And, like most people that make that leap, I had no-idea what I was letting himself in for.

Along the way I spent a regrettably large amount of money on a fancy MBA business degree which temporarily fooled me into thinking I new a LOT more about business than I actually did.

All before getting a rude awakening when I actually started to work for myself and sell stuff in the B2B manufacturing sector through the sales agency company Fibrecore.

In case you're wondering (and depending on when you read this), that 'stuff' was specialist polymer adhesives, industrial flatbed laminating equipment and composite aluminium honeycomb panels.

Sexy, I know.

After having the phone put down on me by what felt like every receptionist, gatekeeper and personal assistant to the managing director at every manufacturing company in the country, I learned a simple strategy for using Linkedin from a fellow salesman at an exhibition in Paris.

And that process formed the foundation for all the results I went on to get from Linkedin in the B2B manufacturing sales sector.

And also for everything you'll learn about how you can get more in-bound leads, warm phone calls and business opportunities from Linkedin in this book.

Before I started to become a big user of Linkedin, I labored under the delusion that finding companies with a potential need for specialist polymer adhesives, industrial flatbed laminating equipment and composite aluminium honeycomb panels was my number one goal.

What I didn't appreciate at first was that if the managing directors, purchasing managers and technical R&D brains at big companies didn't know who I was, like something about me or my products, or trust that I wasn't going to waste their time, the chances of me having a meaningful conversation with them were somewhere between poor and very poor.

I could know the melting point, viscosity and chemical structure of every polymer in our range but if I didn't have that holy sales trilogy of being known, liked and trusted I was on a one-way ticket to sales hell – also known as phone calls, emails and meeting requests that NEVER got answered.

I remember sitting in the Fibrecore office cursing the fact that most of my phone calls to prospects were ending in one of 3 different but equally depressing types of rejection:

- No, we don't take cold calls
- No, we have a no-name policy... and
- No, you'll have to send some information in to our info@ email address

In case you didn't know, the last one is code for: "Our company is far too busy and important to even give you 2 minutes to ask some questions and explain what you sell – please disappear into a black hole, along with the information you send in, which we will NEVER actually look at."

People buy people, not machines or polymers or panels. Sure, these may be the products that get transacted but if the people you're trying to sell to don't like you, they will DEFINITELY find a reason to justify going to a competitor who they do like.

And unless you've invented a time-machine, there is ALWAYS someone with an alternative product.

Everyone who works is too busy to speak to you these days. And getting appointments, introductions and phone calls with the big cheese managers or potential customers you want to speak to can be difficult.

You need an opportunity. You need to get their attention. And you need to stand out from the ocean of other people offering a similar service and ALL claiming they do a better job than the next guy.

Without the right opportunity to get the attention of your ideal prospects, you're like the shy college kid helplessly and hopelessly in love with the high school prom queen.

She is surrounded by muscled-up football jocks. You don't register on her radar. She does not know you exist.

You might love her like no other and be the wittiest, kindest and most awesome boyfriend ever.

But until you get her attention for five minutes, you're never going to the end-of-year ball.

Your ideal customers are also busy. And like everyone out there, they don't like to be sold to.

So you can rely purely on cold calls, sales letters, introductions and referrals – hoping you'll bump into someone who knows someone who works at the company you want to sell to.

Or you can turbo-charge awareness of who you are and how awesome you and your products & services are using social media.

You can stand out from the crowd and quickly get your name known as THE go-to person for water-proof tea bags, inflatable dartboards or whatever it is you sell.

As you'll see over the course of this book, people buy people and Linkedin is a MASSIVELY powerful tool in building relationships with prospective customers – whatever industry or sector they work in.

You don't have to be their best buddy and get an invite to their house for Christmas dinner.

You just need to be known, liked and trusted enough to stand out from the crowd and register on their radar long enough for them to give you a chance.

That's when you'll get those all-important in-bound enquiries, those vital warm phone calls and those shiny new business opportunities.

WANT AN EASIER LIFE?

Would it make your life easier if your sales team was bringing in more business?

My training courses and conference speeches show your sales team exactly how to do just that.

In three easy steps!

Which means they get the know-how they need to become masters of social selling with Linkedin.

And you get a sales team that's getting more in-bound sales leads, more warm phone calls (rather than awkward cold ones) and more business opportunities.

Just check out the testimonials on page 251 to see what some of my recent customers like you think.

Then drop me a message on tom@tommallens.com or a call on +44(0)1926 678 920 to find out how your team could get more leads too.

How social media is changing sales and marketing

WHAT WORKS BEST FOR YOU IN SALES?

Do you have hints or tips that help you beat gatekeepers?

Or specific questions about anything in this book?

Drop me a line on Linkedin or Twitter

And I'll do my best to answer!

www.linkedin.com/in/TomMallens
@TomMallens #GetPastTheGatekeeper

Once upon a time, salespeople were armed with nothing more than a handshake and a way with words to find the right prospects.

They talked and hoped that what they said (and what other people said about them) would get them in front of the right people.

Marketing was about word-of-mouth. And, as a result, what people said mattered. A lot.

Then, in the 15th century, Johannes Gutenberg commercialized the printing press and everything changed.

Marketing as we know it today was born and went from being a purely word-of-mouth affair to being real, tangible, printed material.

The salesman went from having nothing more than words (and the odd hand-written parchment letter) at his disposal to having a vast arsenal of printed marketing material helping him out.

All those good things people might say about you and your products could now potentially be drowned out under an avalanche of printed leaflets, magazines, posters, newspapers, adverts, brochures and flyers shouting at customers about how utterly amazing a particular product was.

And that avalanche only got bigger from there.

In the 20th century, television advertising and e-commerce were born.

Shouting at customers about how great a particular product was turned into screaming at them – from every imaginable angle – and sometimes completely drowning out that powerful word-of-mouth marketing.

Like a skinny rugby player up against a team of 18st bruisers, word-of-mouth was simply being out-muscled.

Mass communication helped companies push products onto customers more aggressively than ever.

And what customers really thought about the products they were buying remained confined to whispered word-of-mouth exchanges between individuals.

That all changed when social media platforms started to emerge in the first few years of the 21st century.

These were simply online platforms where users could exchange information with others in real time.

Suddenly people could communicate not just with the 2, 3 or 10 people in the room with them but with hundreds, thousands or millions of other people around the world.

Word-of-mouth was getting its first injection of steroids. That skinny rugby player had hit the gym, hard. And he was back bigger, stronger and more powerful than ever.

And as you'll see in the rest of this book, that has HUGE implications and opportunities for salespeople like you everywhere.

What is Social Sales anyway?

People do, will and always have bought things from people they know, like and trust.

In some cultures, liking the salesperson you're buying from is almost as important as the product itself – perhaps more so.

People do not like to buy things from people they don't like.

Which is why socialising and building rapport is such a vital part of sales.

Even if you're selling high-tech products and services that are highly differentiated from the competition, if people don't like you they will come up with all kinds of reasons to avoid your phone calls and complicate the sales process to the point where it withers and dies.

If people like you, they will find a stream of new ways to overcome difficulties in the sales process and create a profitable relationship between you both.

Social sales is the art of leveraging your likability to attract more leads and make more sales from socially-minded buyers.

Use this in combination with your other sales tactics, and you have a powerful weapon.

Instead of focusing on the features and benefits of your product or service, social sales is about maximizing the number of people who know, like and trust you – regardless of the product you sell.

In the past, you had to do this by knowing lots of people personally.

Today, you can use social media as a catalyst to exponentially increase the number of people who know, like and trust you.

Not as a replacement for personal, face-to-face relationships but as a way to help you build even more of these valuable and profitable relationships quickly and easily.

You might be able to meet a few people for face-to-face meetings in a day.

But you can be noticed and build rapport with hundreds, thousands or – ultimately – millions of people every day if you use social media effectively.

If these are the right kinds of people (people who could potentially become customers or people who could give you introductions or referrals to these people), then the more of them that know, like and trust you the better.

This will naturally create conversations that build relationships. And those relationships are what will unlock a steady and growing stream of introductions and referrals to the right people.

Unleashing the power of your personal brand

To truly leverage the power of social sales, you must have a personal brand that you can share on social media.

Your brand is the emotions people feel when they think about you.

If you can regularly share updates on social media that reinforce those emotions among your target audience, you have a super-powerful new addition to your box of sales tools.

If people like you, they are more likely to want to do business with you.

In the context of a salesperson, having a powerful and likeable brand can be the difference between key decision makers taking your phone calls and choosing to deliberately ignore you.

Brands are defined in terms of emotions and you must be able to define the emotions you want people to associate with you.

Ask yourself now, what emotions do you want people to feel when they think about you?

Remember, we're talking in a business context here, not a dating website.

Make a note right now. These emotions must be ones that people feel about you. Not about your company and not about your products. They are emotions you want people to feel when they think about you.

If it helps, here are a few examples:

- You want people to feel more successful when they think about you
- You want people to feel more financially secure when they think about you
- You want people to feel happier when they think about you
- You want people to feel more free of worry, stress and fear than they are now
- You want people to feel more certain, purposeful and decisive

- You want people to feel more energized, motivated and positive
- You want people to feel more fashionable, desirable and popular
- You want people to feel more intelligent, astute and insightful

Whatever it is, it helps if it's aligned in some way to what you do.

But more than that it MUST be authentic to who you are.

If you want people to feel more intelligent, astute and insightful it is essential that these are qualities you are genuinely interested in.

You cannot fake this. People can smell insincerity a mile off and they'll quickly get an impression of what you're really like when they meet you face-to-face or speak to you on the phone.

From there, you must reinforce those emotions continually over time.

If people are constantly and gently reminded of who you are, what you do and they like the emotions they feel when they think of you, you will be the person they turn to when they have questions related to your area of expertise.

You will massively increase the number of opportunities and leads you have.

Taking the time to regularly update your social media accounts (whichever platforms you use) and interact with people on them is a powerful way to start making this happen.

If you don't think you have the time for social media. Or if you find yourself wondering if the extra time is worth it, this next bit is for you...

How to enhance your personal brand

Once you know how you want to present yourself to the world, there are a few things you can do to make sure you personal brand is strong and helpful in making sales.

1. Be authentic

Like a politician that's been forced through hundreds of committee meetings into a finely-tuned brand machine, you can shape and mould your personal brand.

But if it's not authentic, you'll never keep up the act.

It will be completely unsustainable and people will feel cheated when they discover what you're really like.

Your personal brand must be built on who you really are.

This includes your likes, inclinations, habits, strengths, how you like to dress and beyond.

There are some things in life you can fake until you make. Your personal brand is not one of them.

2. Match your work to your brand

Once you've figured out who you are and how you want to be, you need to make sure it's going to help you in your job – and be appropriate for the work you do.

Notice that your brand comes first, then you can go and find the work that allows and rewards you for the qualities you naturally display.

If you work out who you are and then try to force it into the job you do, it may be like trying to fit a square peg into a round hole.

It just won't work.

Get it right, and you'll be able to thrive by being yourself!

3. Be known for something

Everyone with a strong personal brand is known for something.

And to really shine, it's essential that people instantly associate you with something.

For maximum impact, this should be something that separates you from everyone else and makes you stand out from the crowd.

Remember, you cannot be known for everything. If you are, you're fundamentally known for nothing. You have then become a Z-list reality TV celeb.

Be known for one thing and you'll be the go-to person that people call when they have a problem that you can solve.

4. Behave true to your brand

Whatever you're known for, the most important thing is that you behave in a way that's consistent with it.

People can smell inauthenticity a mile away and they distrust it.

People absolutely trust people they feel are authentic.

It's why people often respect people that they don't particularly like.

The person they don't like is completely authentic and true to their brand so even if they don't like them, they know what they're dealing with and respect them for it.

5. Spread the word

Of course, your personal brand will spread much quicker if you reinforce it at every stage possible.

This means making sure your marketing material, both online and offline, reflects and spreads your brand.

A great way to test this is to Google yourself and see what comes up in the first few pages.

This is exactly what many potential customers will be doing so it's vital that you do the same, see what the results are and work to improve them as much as possible.

I'm already busy - is social selling worth bothering with?

Whatever you do in life, it's unlikely you're the only one doing it.

We live in a competitive world and you will almost certainly have competitors, whether they're direct competitors with the same products and services or indirect ones with alternative things your potential customers can buy.

In either case, it is increasingly difficult to be leagues ahead of your competition.

Information and ideas move too quickly to hold on to big advantages for months or years.

If you have a unique product, someone, somewhere will probably be working on an alternative version of it to launch into the market.

It's not world-changing differences that allow some people to be more successful than others. It's slight advantages that accumulate over time to become unassailable leads.

Rugby World Cup-winning manager Clive Woodward summed up his approach to beating the dominant teams in the world – like New Zealand and Australia – not as trying to out-perform them by miles in any one area (that was just about impossible).

Instead, he focused on doing 50 things, just half a percent better than them.

Added together, that creates a BIG advantage: One that allowed the England rugby team to win the World Cup in 2003.

Over and over again, it's slight advantages that help put people on the road to success.

By sheer luck, Bill Gates had access to a state-of-the-art computer lab during his childhood in the 1960s and 1970s.

Hardly any other potentially equally gifted programmers of his generation would have had the same access.

The Beatles found work playing 8-hour sets in the strip clubs of Hamburg where they were required to play everything from jazz to hard rock.

Very few equally creative up-and-coming bands would have been able to earn a living while simultaneously practicing, experimenting and improving their musical skills.

In youth ice hockey teams in Canada, children born late in the calendar year are put into the same leagues as children born early in the calendar, according to the academic year.

Their slight head-start in size and physical strength means they perform slightly better which gradually gets reinforced with better results, selection for the top teams, increased confidence and more attention from the best youth coaches.

In every case, just a very slight advantage at the start, is compounded over time to produce significantly better results until the people in question are streets ahead of the competition.

MORNING MOTIVATION

One of the best ways to start the day is with something positive, and uplifting that pushes you to take action towards your goals. Remember, these MUST be written down if you want to achieve them. If they're not written down, they don't count!

For the last 3 years (ish), I've published a motivational quote on Linkedin (and Twitter and Facebook) every morning. Here are some of the most popular 8AM INSPIRATION quotes to keep you on track to achieving your sales goals.

What words of wisdom get you motivated for a great day every morning? Let me know . . . @TomMallens #8AMINSPIRATION

"Fear is a prison, where you are the jailer. Free yourself!"
– **Bryant McGill**

"I didn't fail the test. I just found 100 ways to do it wrong."
– **Benjamin Franklin**

"Once you choose hope, anything's possible." – **Christopher Reeve**

"The difference between who you are and who you want to be is what you do." – **Bill Phillips**

"In order to succeed, your desire for success should be greater than your fear of failure." – **Bill Cosby**

"If you change the way you look at things, the things you look at change." – **Dr Wayne Dyer**

"Live out of your imagination, not your history." – **Stephen Covey**

"Your life does not get better by chance. It gets better by change."
– **Jim Rohn**

From the Yellow Pages to Richard Branson and beyond

Just as slight advantages have changed the fortunes of international business superstars and sports teams, exactly the same thing can happen to you and your sales.

If you start building social media and social selling into your regular routine, you'll start to out-perform your competitors.

Perhaps only by half a percent at first but as those stories illustrate, that's how everyone that ever got ahead started – by being just half a percent better.

Slight advantages get compounded over time, building confidence and reputation, until the salesperson in question outperforms others in the same field.

In a survey of 3,094 sales professionals (including reps, managers and consultants) by strategy consultant Jill Konrath, it was found that only 4.9% of people took full advantage of Linkedin as a sales tool.

This 4.9% said the bulk of their new leads and opportunities came from using Linkedin.

39.4% of the sales people surveyed said they uncovered "several opportunities" from the platform.

However, more than half of the people questioned said they didn't generate any new business from Linkedin.

When asked why, they said it was because they believed it was mainly a job-hunting site.

Research by Jim Keenan has shown that salespeople who regularly use social media sell more than their colleagues.

72.6% of sales people using social media as part of their sales process outperform their sales peers and exceed quota 23% more often.

The results of the surveys show that many salespeople are missing out on the 'slight edges' that would help them pull ahead of their peers.

In fact, there are several ways social media – and Linkedin in particular – can help salespeople at different points of the sales cycle.

And it's precisely those that we'll be investigating in this book.

Social media is changing EVERYTHING when it comes to sales.

Because suddenly, you have the potential to find, interact and socialize with almost anyone you want to in business.

And socialising with people creates relationships. Relationships open doors that were previously locked to you. And these open doors are the gateways to new opportunities (providing you walk through them and, even better, walk through the right ones).

It strikes me as odd that while many of the biggest entrepreneurial and sales names on the planet – from Richard Branson to Brian Tracy to Brad Sugars and Robert Kiyosaki – embrace social media to spread word-of-mouth awareness of them and their products, many considerably less well off, less successful and less well-known business people continue to turn their noses up at social media.

If it's good enough for Richard Branson and Brian Tracy, I suspect it's good enough for most sales people.

Often, the problem is that people don't truly understand the power of it.

If the Yellow Pages was the go-to business marketing resource of the past, websites are the essential business marketing resource of the present.

And social media is the business marketing resource of the future.

The reason I say that is because all the signs indicate that social media has not come anywhere close to its full potential.

There are still VAST and untapped opportunities for social media to be integrated into the lives of consumers, business people, marketers and sales professionals.

I believe what we've seen from social media (a bit of Facebook, Linkedin and Twitter here and there) is just the tip of the iceberg.

There are college campuses in the US that no longer issue students with email addresses.

They communicate and conduct all their business and administrative activities through social media.

There is a generation of future managers and sales superstars entering the workplace right now who do not use email as their default means of communicating with people they can't speak to face-to-face or on the phone.

For the new generation of sales professionals, social media is simply how you communicate with people that aren't sat in front of you or on the other end of the phone.

Greeting, meeting and (eventually) eating!

The best methods of building rapport with a prospect currently go in the following order (from best to worst)

- **Face-to-face meeting with food** – If you're eating with someone, relationships form 10 times faster than if you're not!

- **Face-to-face meeting** – Getting in front of people remains the best way to build rapport and make sure your communication is effective.

- **Video call** – You may be on the other side of the world but video calls combine the benefits of face-to-face meetings with the speed and convenience of phone calls.

- **Phone call** – All other things being equal, the more of the right kinds of people you speak to in business the better. The phone is the quickest way of getting high-quality interaction with people.

- **Personal letter** – In a world where most decision makers are overloaded with emails, a well-written letter will almost always get opened. You will get the attention of the person you want to speak to.

- **Email or text** – Quick and simple but frighteningly easy for people to ignore or claim they never saw (err, it went into my spam folder, honest!).

The more you can communicate with potential prospects using the methods above, the better. Traditionally, you wanted as much of that communication to be face-to-face or on the phone as possible.

Why? Because the more high-quality time you can spend building relationships with prospects and valuable contacts the better. And relationships develop on the basis of high-quality time spent together.

It's very hard to develop good relationships with someone on email.

People are tactile creatures. It's why we say 'keep in touch'. Notice no-one ever says 'keep in hearing' or 'keep in electronic images on my screen'.

If you're serious about developing good relationships with existing and potential customers, you should always be looking for ways to move up that list from distant electronic forms of communication to closer, face-to-face forms of communication.

However, as you're reading this, the structure of that list is changing. There is a new player in town that can help you achieve your goal of getting more personal communication.

That new player is social media.

Social media is slotting in right underneath phone calls as a much more powerful way to build rapport and establish relationships than texts or emails.

Like phone calls (and unlike letters) social media is about personal two-way engagement in real-time.

Emails and texts are much less engaging because they lack that feeling of personal one-to-one contact.

How many times have you instantly deleted a sales email from someone you didn't know?

If you're anything like me, it's probably a lot.

Social media let's you communicate on a personal level in a way that's less sales-like and much harder to ignore, dismiss or delete.

At the most basic level, you communicate on social media with a photo of you next to everything you say. That might seem like a small point but it's extremely important.

People feel on a subconscious level that they're engaging with you personally.

And that creates more personal engagement, which is the foundation of better quality relationships.

It makes it easier to progress up the list from the impersonal and bland email to the highly personal and relationship-building phone call, meeting and eating.

Social media is also a powerful way of finding the people you want to speak to.

If you use it effectively, there's no need to wait for that long-lost colleague to make an introduction to a potential customer for a meeting.

Instead, you can go out there and find the people you want to speak to and start interacting with them straight away!

This is HUGE.

You don't have to wait any longer. The potential for instant results is right there in front of you.

But more than this, rather than relying on social media as a means to get your marketing messages in front of the right people, you can use them for what they were designed to do all along; socialise.

My understanding of this was transformed after I met Bernie De Souza, a master in the methods of landing new clients.

Clearing up the big social media myths

This new opportunity for communication on a massive scale through social media brings scores of advantages but it's not a magic panacea.

There are so many misconceptions about social media and social selling that it's worth addressing them before we move on.

Myth 1. Good social media makes up for a bad product

If you're product is bad, I'm afraid you're still screwed. All the talking to people on social media in the world isn't going to help if your product stinks; in the same way that talking to lots of people face-to-face won't stop them realising the truth that your products actually don't do what you claim.

Social media is a powerful way to spread what people are already saying about you and/or your products. It's a way to add fuel to the fire of word-of-mouth marketing and referrals.

If people are saying good things, you can encourage those messages to spread to new audiences and potential customers more quickly.

If they're saying bad things, you can use social media to understand why and what they have issues with more quickly and effectively.

Myth 2. Social media is the only marketing you need to do

Social media is not a magic button that can replace your other sales or marketing strategies.

If someone tells you they're only doing social media to promote their business or make sales, then I'd be extremely worried about their business.

Some of the best social media companies out there do HUGE amounts of other marketing, from networking and leaflet drops to radio advertising and direct mail.

Why? Social media is a hugely powerful marketing channel but it is only one marketing channel. And the best marketing covers multiple channels.

The synergy happens in the interplay of different sales and marketing strategies.

In the same way that two horses working together can pull more than double the weight of one horse working on its own, 10 well organized marketing channels working together will create more than 10 times the impact of each individual channel working independently.

Social media is an accelerator. If you're a chemist, it's a catalyst to speed up the effectiveness of your other marketing activities.

But a catalyst on its own does nothing. Social media on its own is just noise.

Myth 3. Social media is free

That's right. Social media is NOT free marketing. Why? Because like everything in business it takes time. And time is money.

It may be free to sign-up for an account with Linkedin, Twitter, Facebook or Google+ but to get results you need to invest time in using them.

If you don't actually do anything with them, they won't do anything for you.

Getting results from social media is about taking time to build up relationships with people that are relevant to you and your sales activities in particular.

And relationships take time. Some relationships are faster than others but generally, the more time involved, the better the relationship.

The slower the burn, the longer the relationship lasts. And that goes for relationships with customers too.

Myth 4. Social media delivers instant results (with one BIG caveat)

Social media and social selling will not make you a millionaire overnight. Despite what you may have heard, it will not mean you instantly make sales with anyone you find or follow online.

Success comes from the right kind of action, taken in large amounts and done consistently over time.

It's then that you'll start moving towards the front of the sales success queue with more in-bound leads, more warm (rather than cold) phone calls and more business opportunities.

This is an almost natural result of becoming better known and liked within your industry by prospects and creating an understanding that you are the go-to expert in your field.

If you go charging in to a prospect, it's make or break time. They'll either buy from you, not buy from you or – as is often the case when you don't get your pitch quite right – procrastinate endlessly and never take a decision either way.

Relationships that you cultivate over time tend to be much more productive in business terms as a result. And social media is a powerful tool to help you do this.

That BIG caveat I mentioned...

Where Linkedin differs considerably from Facebook and Twitter is that it's much easier to get 'instant' results when it comes to sales.

There is such a HUGE amount of information about your prospects on Linkedin that just logging in once and looking in the right places can give you the vital knowledge or rapport-building information you need to make a difference.

Sometimes this is who your prospect knows that can give you that introduction or referral you've been desperately looking for.

And sometimes it's a name or piece of rapport-building information that will get you past a gatekeeper or receptionist and create a better relationship within seconds of your phone call.

Either way, as mentioned at the start of this section, social media will help you gain a sales edge over your competitors and over time, that edge can become insurmountable.

By becoming better known, liked and trusted by the right people in your industry, you can begin your journey to becoming the go-to person everyone talks about and turns to when they need advice and information about anything related to the products and services you sell.

If you are, then let me know on Linkedin or Twitter and I'll see how I can help best!

@TomMallens

A SECRET THAT MIGHT SHOCK YOU

I'd like to tell you a secret. One that transformed how I think about marketing.

And skyrocketed the results I got in business.

I learnt it from an interesting man called Stefan, who I bumped into at an otherwise pretty forgettable and grey networking event.

It was the secret of writing more persuasively.

So that anyone reading what you write is more likely to read it all. And then, actually do what you ask at the end.

If you can write words that sell effectively, and speak persuasively in front of people too, then you've got a winning combination.

And you tend to sell a lot more in the process.

If you sign-up for my emails at
www.tommallens.com/moreleadsfromlinkedin
then you'll learn how to write words that do your selling for you.

And loads of other invaluable stuff too.

Which means you'll make your job easier and get better results as well.

It's free. And it only takes 30 seconds.

Just go to www.tommallens.com/moreleadsfromlinkedin now.

Some lead generation revision!

WANT TO GET MORE SALES LEADS?

There's one surprising thing you can do that will improve your sales results.

It's completely free.

It works on anyone.

And you can use it any time to improve your results.

People do business with people they like.

And what's the easiest way to make more people take a liking to you?

Smile!

The more you smile, the happier people feel around you.

And the happier people feel, the more likely they are to want to work with you.

Give it a try today!

As we've seen, people do business with people they know, like and trust and you can use social media to build each of these three qualities in the minds of prospects and useful contacts.

But how does that help you get more leads and make more sales exactly?

First of all, it's helpful to clarify what we mean when we talk about leads.

Leads are potential customers that you have communicated with.

More specifically, and firstly, they are people that match the criteria of one of your target markets.

In other words, they have a potential desire for your product and the means to pay for it.

And secondly, there has been some communication.

They have contacted you OR you have contacted them and had a response.

Whether this response is positive or negative, it doesn't really matter! Remember, if people have objections, it actually means they're interested. If they're totally indifferent, they'll ignore you.

If they have objections, it means they have an opinion about your offer and now that they've explained their objection, you have the information you need to overcome that objection.

If they don't object, you have nothing to go on.

In that sense, objections are great news. In fact, start to feel happy when people give you objections. Objections are just opportunities in disguise.

In traditional lead-finding and sales, the process was all about three things:

1. Identifying and finding the right potential customers
2. Getting their attention and putting a compelling offer in front of them
3. Giving them a reason not to delay but to take action now

Having found the right people and got their attention with your offer, you're free to move those prospects down the sales pipeline towards a decision.

Let's take a moment to review those areas. As we'll see shortly, even if you use social media to become better known, like and trusted by prospects, it's still essential that you have a robust offer behind the socialising to back it up.

If you just socialise on social media without a great offer to back it up, you're not doing business, you're just making a lot of noise.

Finding the right potential customers

In the same way that certain types of people are more likely to buy from you than others, there are certain types of people that are more valuable to you on social media.

Not everyone out there will become a potential customer of yours.

And not everyone you connect with on social media will either.

In general, the people it is most worth connecting with on social media fall into one of three categories:

• Potential customers
• Referral partners
• Industry influencers

Let's take a quick look at those in more detail.

Potential customers

These are people that match the profile of your ideal customer.

You can often find them on social media through intelligent use of search criteria focused on specific keywords.

If you know the interests, activities, skills or qualifications that your potential customers are most likely to have, you will be able to search for them on Linkedin, Twitter, Facebook and Google+.

As we'll see in a second, you're then in a position to bring these people into your network and nurture relationships with them.

To be absolutely sure who you're ideal target customer is, it's a great idea to give yourself a clear picture of what they look like.

If you go online, you can use a photo-fit image generator to create a picture of exactly what your ideal target customer looks like.

You can then more easily tailor all your marketing, emails and written communications directly to them in a way that will appeal to them.

It also keeps you focused on looking out for people that match your ideal customer demographic.

HAVE YOU SEEN THIS MAN?

Brian Middleton is wanted for social sales training. Brian is 54 years old. He is sales manager at a manufacturing company in the Midlands. Brian could help his team get more leads more easily and more often if they spent just 3.5 hours learning how to use Linkedin in an effective way, without making the mistakes most salespeople make that stop them getting a steady stream of leads and referrals.

Call +44 (0)1926 678 920 NOW to help Brian master social sales and get more leads!

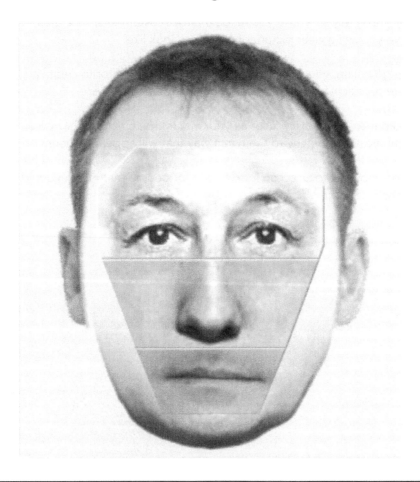

Referral partners

Using social media to look for potential referral partners is an extremely good use of your time.

Referral partners are people with a non-competing interest in the same target market as you.

In other words, they are people with products and services that your ideal customers might want to buy as well as (and NOT instead of) your products and services.

These people are sometimes known as 'joint venture partners' or 'strategic allies'.

Whatever you call them, building relationships with referral partners is extremely valuable and important because it's a win-win for all parties.

You can pass business to each other without any fear that you will compromise the demand for your own products.

Examples of referral partners can include:

- A wedding planner and a florist
- A business consultant and a training provider
- A health & safety specialist and an insurance company
- An IT hardware company and a software specialist
- Material suppliers producing materials for a single production process

By finding these people on social media, you can start to build relationships and look for mutually beneficial opportunities to pass business to each other.

Industry influencers

Whatever industry you work in there are some people for whom the doors of opportunity always seem open. Let's call them 'industry influencers'.

These people tend to be well-connected and know exactly who to speak to get ahead.

Perhaps they're heads of trade associations, they sit on the board of several companies, or they act as a highly-paid consultant and thought-leader.

Whatever they do, these are people that it is definitely worth knowing if you want to start to out-perform your competitors.

It may be hard to get one-to-one time with them at first, so Linkedin is a great place to find them and gradually build up a relationship.

If you're in regular contact with these people on Linkedin, you start to open up all kinds of new possibilities as you begin to get to know them.

Now that you've found some of the right potential customers, it's time to move onto step two of the traditional methods of lead-finding.

It's time to develop a great offer that will get prospects' attention and help you get more leads.

Remember that no matter what the industry or sector, a great offer has certain key characteristics:

Components of a compelling offer 1: Benefits

First and foremost, a great offer contains a clear explanation of the benefits to the end-user.

It may sound obvious but it amazes me how often people miss this. A great offer must contain a benefit for the potential customer.

It's not enough just to explain the features your product offers. You must be able to explain the benefits these features deliver for your target market quickly and concisely.

These benefits must be appealing to your ideal target customers.

And for maximum social sales success you must be able to sum them up in the length of one social media status update.

The good news is, depending on the platform, this is about one or two short sentences.

So if you can answer people quickly and concisely when they ask 'what do you do?', then you can fit this into the length of a Linkedin status update too.

Benefits generally boil down to either helping people make money or save money.

But try to be more specific than this. The more specific and relevant to your ideal target market you can be about the benefits you offer the better.

Does your product help reduce post-production labour costs in textile businesses? Or does it save time and effort in bookkeeping so that data-input clerks have more time to take on other more profitable tasks within a business?

It's amazing how many people in B2B sales say 'I sell printing machinery' or 'I sell cloud computing solutions' and completely fail to mention any kind of benefit.

They assume that just because they know and understand the benefits their products offer that everyone else will too.

Alternatively, they make the benefits so generic as to be almost meaningless.

Saying that 'our Turbo-tron X500 machine has a new Eco-Boost button which saves you money' is so vague it's almost meaningless.
If you can explain that the new Eco-Boost button reduces the unit's power consumption by 31% which means that users get electricity bills that are an average of £4,700 per year lower, that starts to become a much more compelling offer.

Components of a compelling offer 2: Certainty

Great offers must contain an element of certainty. That is, the understanding that if someone takes up the offer, it is CERTAIN they will get the benefits.

When you explain the feature a particular product has, you must follow this with the benefit that this AUTOMATICALLY results in.

People like to know exactly what they're getting when they buy things.

Any uncertainty creates fear. And fear is one of the major obstacles to buying.

People may love the benefits you offer but not be certain that they will receive them if they purchase.

When you describe the features your product offers, always follow this with the phrase 'which means that you . . . ' and then explain the benefit.

You must remind people what your benefits are AND that those benefits are an INEVITABLE result of the features your product has.

One way to communicate that certainty is to offer a guarantee.

For example: "Our warehouse has the largest range of screw fittings in the country and the fastest picking and delivery times, which means purchasing managers always get the screw fittings they need delivered within 36 hours of order, guaranteed or their next delivery is free".

One of the great things about guarantees is that as well as creating certainty for the potential customer, they force you to raise your game.

If you start offering a guarantee that deliveries will be at the customer within 36 hours of order, you'll be amazed how quickly your company finds a way to make this happen.

If you just try to deliver within 36 hours without a guarantee to back it up, there will be a lot more deliveries coming in at 37 and 38 hours.

There's no reason for your delivery team to go the extra mile.

And while your customers might be OK with 37 hours, they won't have any certainty that delivery will be within 37 hours.

What about those times when deliveries run over to 39, 42 or 50 hours? That's when they'll have problems.

Without a guarantee, the fear that these problems may occur may put people off buying from you, especially if there's a company that's guaranteed the delivery times on their service nearby.

Components of a compelling offer 3: A reason to take action

Now that you've found the right people (those who want your product and have the ability to pay), and explained the benefits, it's important to give them a reason to take action.

As explained above, we've got a great offer in front of the right people and that offer is loaded with benefits for the customer and certainty that those benefits will inevitably follow.

But there's still one piece of the jigsaw missing. We need to give people a reason to take action.

Without a reason to take action, you risk falling into that horrible place where prospects don't say yes or no to you.

Instead, they simply don't take a decision.

Which leaves you constantly chasing them and wasting time when you could be focusing your sales energy on people who will let you know if they want to buy or not.

In that sense, sales rejection is good!

It means you can move on to a prospect who may be very keen to buy from you.

The best way to avoid this indecision is to build a reason to take action into your sales offer from the start and make it an integral part of your sales pitch.

Great ways to get people to stop procrastinating and take action include:

Give them a deadline
If people don't have a reason to take a decision, they will naturally avoid taking one.

Decisions mean change and change holds the possibility of getting into a worse situation than the one the prospect is already in.

To avoid this, you can force the issue by making them take a decision.

If you make a compelling offer, explain that it expires by a given time and date.

If they don't decide to benefit from your offer by X o'clock on whatever date, the passage of time will take the decision for them and they'll miss out by default.

Get them using your products and services for free
If someone is already using your products and services, it becomes extremely easy to get them to pay for it. Psychologically, they're already a customer (they're just not a paying customer... yet!).

Once you've explained the features and benefits you deliver to the specific kind of person with a guarantee that they'll inevitably experience the benefits, explain that they might as well give it a try at no cost and with no obligation.

This free product or service could be a small sample for testing purposes or a scaled-down version of the full paid-for product.

Either way, it's a simple way to get the prospect to keep taking decisions and move them down the sales pipeline.

Give them a no-risk way out
People don't like to make mistakes. Whatever anyone tells you about how mistakes are a great source of learning, people would rather avoid them in the first place.

In fact, most business coaches will tell you that there are no such things as mistakes, only 'opportunities to learn from'.

While I do personally believe this is 100% true. It doesn't mean I or anyone else actively wants to attract mistakes if they can be avoided.

If they happen, you can choose to get miserable OR you can choose to learn from them and begin again stronger and better informed.

But most people would rather avoid them in the first place.

And one of the big mistakes people want to avoid is buying stuff they don't actually want or need.

If you can remove the fear that this will happen, it becomes much easier to get people to take a decision and move forward by trying or buying your products.

One way to remove this fear is to give them a no-risk way out.

Explain that if they're not happy after they buy the product or service, they can return it or get a refund without any hassle, quibbles or problems.

Just like the guarantee we discussed earlier, once you offer this no-risk way out, you'll find you suddenly go the extra mile to make sure your customers ARE happy after they buy.

You'll speak to them more, reassure them more and ask more questions to better understand their needs.

Be a consultant, not a sales person
Offering people no-risk ways out so they don't feel the fear of making a wrong decision is a massively powerful tactic.

It's so powerful and helpful that you may want to build it into the whole way you position yourself in the eyes of prospects.

Explain that you're job is not to sell anything. You job is simply to find out which products or services might help someone the most for free.

Then, if it's not exactly the right option for your prospect that will INEVITABLY lead to the benefits they're looking for, they pay nothing and go away having benefitted from a clearer picture of exactly what they do want.

If people are afraid of making wrong decisions, they try to avoid taking any and instead stick with the status quo.

By reassuring people from the start that your job is not to sell but to listen to their needs and see if you can help or not, you make it much easier for them to take action.

And action is essential to that three-step process of getting more leads we discussed: 1. Identify and find the right people 2. Give them a compelling offer 3. Give them a reason to take action!

Explain the perils of the status quo
As we discussed, fear of taking the wrong decision is a big reason prospects don't take decisions about your products and services and, instead, stick with the status quo.

You can remove the fear of taking the wrong decision by offering them a risk-free way out after they've bought and by positioning yourself as a consultant (rather than a salesperson) before they've bought.

You can also explain how sticking with the status quo and not giving your product or service a try is a much less attractive option than they realised.

If people do what they've always done, they'll get what they've always got.

So unless your prospect is 100% happy with where they are right now, then in fact, the status quo is not where they want or need to be.

How do you find out if your prospect is happy or not? By asking questions; lots of open-ended questions!

Those are the 5 ways I've found most effective in getting people to stop procrastinating and take a decision about buying or not.

Speaking of 5, I'd like to share another 5 things with you before we get into the social sales stuff.

These are 5 steps to making a sale. I've found them MASSIVELY helpful in structuring my thinking to make my sales more effective.

The idea goes that there are only five stages to every sale. They are:

1. Identifying prospects and building rapport
2. Finding stuff out
3. Checking the facts
4. Making a proposal
5. Asking for the order

That's it. Just five steps. Let's have a quick look at them in more detail.

Identifying prospects and building rapport
This is where it all starts. And it's a phase that Linkedin can help with in a HUGE way by helping you get past gatekeepers and contact people direct.

People do business with people they like. And more specifically, they tend to do business with people like them.

By being liked, you don't make a sale. But you give yourself the chance to lay the foundations for a sale.

If people don't like you, they won't buy. Full stop.

Whether it's on the phone, face-to-face or on Linkedin, you MUST make a conscious effort to build rapport.

Perhaps you need to be friendly, perhaps you need to be fast and to-the-point. In almost every case, you probably just need to show a side of yourself that's a bit more like the person you're speaking to.

If you ignore this stage and start trying to get down to assessing a customers needs too quickly, the sale will almost NEVER go anywhere.

Rapport is vital. So don't ignore it. Depending on the industry you're in (and particularly in the service sector), sales can happen ONLY because of rapport.

Sometimes, people will simply buy from you because they like you and buying is a natural way to enhance your relationship.

Finding stuff out
Now that you've created some rapport, you're in a position to find some stuff about your prospect out.

How do you do this? By asking questions! And crucially, they should be open questions.

This is the phase where you want your prospect to talk. LOTS.

Open questions cannot be answered with a yes or a no. And they start with one of the following words:

- How
- Where
- When
- Who
- Why
- What

Most people like to talk about themselves, their challenges, problems, ideas and opportunities.

So give them the space to get talking. Focus on finding out where they are now, where they want to get to and why it is they're not there already – in other words, what's holding them back.

If you're ever stuck for a question and don't know what to say next, you can ALWAYS fall back on the trusty three words: "Why is that?".

The more you ask it, the more you find out about what your prospect is REALLY thinking.

Which is the key to delivering an irresistible solution that they will want to buy.

Checking the facts
Now that you've deployed the open questions, it's time to switch to the closed ones.

Before you make a proposal, you want to be as sure as possible that they'll want to buy it.

This is where you can clarify and confirm EVERYTHING and eliminate any objections BEFORE they happen.

Go through everything they told you during your questions to find stuff out and ask them to confirm that you understand them correctly.

Now that you know the facts, you can decide whether your product or service really is what your prospect wants or needs.

If you believe you can help them, you can move onto stage four of the five-step process.

If you don't believe your product is right, then you don't have to do any selling at all; you've built up great rapport and found out lots of stuff that you can use to help that person in the future, help them by referring them to someone else or suggesting some other ideas.

But if their problems DO match your solutions, then you can move to step 4...

Make a proposal
Armed with all the information, you can now explain – in person or in writing – what you can do to solve their problems once and for all.

Focus on explaining how they will benefit from your services. How will life be better if they buy from you?

If you've gone through steps 1, 2 and 3 fully, they should be completely sold on the idea you suggest as it will be exactly the thing they're looking for.

If they're not, it is probably because you didn't dig deep enough with your questions or build enough rapport at the start.

Ask for the order
Finally, you need to actually ask for the business. If you don't ask, you probably won't get.

Rather than saying: "Do you want to buy it?". A great alternative is: "Why don't you give it a try?".

This is much softer and makes people much less worried about the decision they've just made to buy.

After all, they're now not buying. They're just giving it a try.

The result is exactly the same. But how your prospect feels about it will be very different.

If you don't make a sale in a given situation, it's usually because you've rushed to point 5 either too quickly or too late.

If you ask for the business too soon, you don't have any rapport with the prospect and you probably don't have a full understanding of their situation and whether you can help or not.

A lot of people don't actually ever get to point 5 and ask for the business.

Even if you get a no, at least you have a decision.

You can then move on and don't have to invest more time in a person who is very unlikely to buy.

I've found those 5 points extremely helpful in structuring my sales. And I hope you do too!

Just remember, these are foundation sales and lead-finding techniques.

What we're really here to talk about is the power of social selling and how it can help you get ahead.

So how does traditional lead finding and sales compare with a social media-based approach?

Getting past gatekeepers through social selling

Traditional lead-finding is all about getting a compelling offer in front of the right people with a reason to take action now.

Those three things absolutely still apply and you should make them a big focus of your sales activities.

But now, those strategies have been enhanced with the ability to use social media to do something previously only reserved for people you could meet face-to-face; to become:

- Better known
- Better liked and
- Better trusted...

... by as many of the right kinds of people, potential customers and key influencers on Linkedin as possible.

And not just by one or two but potentially by hundreds, thousands and tens of thousands, without any gatekeepers getting in the way.

The great thing about Linkedin as a social media platform for sales people is that it makes it easy to find the right kinds of people and become known by them; to build likability and rapport with those people; and to develop trust through a consistent presence where you are seen as credible and worth listening to.

There is no longer a cast-iron barrier between the people in an organization that you want to speak to and you as the salesman or woman looking in.

That cast-iron barrier guarded by marauding gate-keepers ready to shoot you down has been replaced by a porous barrier of social media platforms like Linkedin.

You log in, find the people you want to speak to and then get to work building rapport on a personal level.

Social media platforms like Linkedin mean the idea of business-to-business sales is changing.

Businesses don't sell to businesses anymore. People sell to people.

B2B has become P2P.

TRADITIONAL SALES & SOCIAL SALES

TRADITIONAL	SOCIAL
Pushes out information about products and services	Generates in-bound interest in products and services
Focusses on relevant companies	Focusses on relevant people
Looks for chances to pitch and close	Discovers, nurtures and creates relationships

Becoming known, liked and trusted by your prospects

Social media creates huge opportunities for the salesperson who's prepared to master the art of becoming better known, liked and trusted online.

Becoming known is about using the social media platforms themselves to get your message to the right people.

Whether it's Linkedin, Facebook, Twitter, Google+ or YouTube, understanding the features of each platform will help you more precisely target the exact demographics of people who best match your ideal customer profile.

Becoming known on social media with a view to achieving social sales success is all about building a network of contacts.

It's those contacts that will provide that stream of referrals, introductions and word-of-mouth recommendations that will create new opportunities and profitable relationships for you.

The best part is, those people will WANT to do it for you. Why? Because they know you, like you and trust you.

And people do business with people they know, like and trust.

There are 3 key areas to focus on in building your network of contacts and thereby increasing the number of people who know you.

These steps are fundamentally the same no-matter what social media platform you're on.

1. Connecting with people you already know

The best place to start building your network on any social media platform is with the people you already know.

If you already speak to them in business, make it even easier to keep in contact by connecting with them online.

This fulfills two functions: It helps you communicate quickly and easily with the people who are most important to you in business. And (particularly on Linkedin), it lets you see who your close contacts know who could also be useful contacts or prospects for you.

If you approach someone cold and try to make a sale, you've got a lesser chance of success than if you get an introduction to them from one of your mutual close friends.

Creating a community of contacts around you and providing an easy place to talk and interact with you is a great first step to leveraging your personal brand.

In this case, social media creates an easy place for people to communicate with you and gives you an easy place to constantly reinforce your brand with the people you already know.

Most of the platforms (including Linkedin, Twitter, Facebook and Google+) provide a way for you to organize your contacts.

Linkedin calls it 'tagging', Twitter calls them 'lists' and Google+ calls them 'circles'.

Whatever the platform, the idea is the same. You can communicate with all the people in your network or you can target communications to a particular sub-section that you define in a way that is right for you.

Creating tags, lists or circles is ideally something you should start doing from the beginning. Although in either case, the best time to start is now!

To get started, think about your top 5 different types of customer and give each type a name.

Then create Linkedin tags based on these names.

Moving forward, you can then communicate in a much more targeted and effective way with the people you know in business.

2. Connecting with people you meet face-to-face

Have you ever met someone that could be a really useful contact and then not got in touch again for months or even years?

I know I have.

Sometimes they were extremely useful contacts that could have been a big help for the future.

But because contact wasn't maintained, getting in touch out of the blue when you want something can become awkward and full of difficulties to negotiate in re-establishing the relationship.

That all stopped when I started getting into the habit of connecting with new people I met on social media.

It's an extremely valuable thing to do because it makes it MUCH easier to maintain relationships for the future.

But don't just stop there with adding people you meet on Linkedin or other platforms.

Encourage people you meet or who read about you to come to you first!

That means including calls to action on your marketing material encouraging people to find you on Linkedin and/or other social media platforms and giving them a BENEFIT for doing so.

Marketing material includes, but is not limited to the following:

- Business cards
- Brochures
- Flyers and leaflets
- Websites
- Emails

On each of these items, include a call to action asking people to find and connect with you on social media together with a benefit.

This benefit could be a specific gift, offer or type of information. Alternatively, it could simply be something fun or light-hearted that will entertain people.

Here are a few examples:

- Connect on Linkedin for the latest news from the hydraulic pump industry
- Find me on Linkedin for the 5 fastest ways to save up to 48% on your fleet management costs
- Follow me on Twitter for the latest opinions on cloud storage solutions
- Like me on Facebook for exclusive ways to out-source your company's HR
- Find me on Linkedin and see who I know that you'd like an introduction to!
- Get in touch on Google+ to see how me and the PowerClean team keep commercial caterers like you happy – GUARANTEED!

Notice that these calls to action (and reasons to do so) range from the fairly formal to the more fun and light-hearted.

Social sales is about leveraging your personal brand.

For that reason, crafting one that's in keeping with you and how you behave in business is vital if your brand is going to be consistent and, therefore, powerful.

If you're a larger-than-life character, it makes sense for you to have a larger-than-life personal brand, with larger-than-life social media updates and activities.

If people like your social media activity online they they're going to LOVE you when they meet you in person.

Likewise, if people don't like your style when you're on social media, they're probably not going to like you much when you meet.

So you might as well get that hurdle out of the way to start with.

People buy from people they know, like and trust so let as many people as possible know what you're like and the ones that like you will naturally be drawn to you and your business offer.

3. Connecting with new prospects you've not met... yet!

The final stage of using Linkedin to become better known by more of the right kinds of people to help you in your sales is to connect with new prospects you've not met yet – a great way to get past gatekeepers.

No matter what platform you're using, this means understanding and using the search facilities to find new potential customers you haven't met or interacted with.

You can then use Linkedin (or any other platform) to build rapport and help turn this stranger into an engaged and enthusiastic potential customer who not only knows you but likes you and trusts you too.

There's plenty more to come on this subject in the rest of this book.

MORNING MOTIVATION

"A man is a success if he gets up in the morning and gets to bed at night and in between does what he wants to do." – **Bob Dylan**

"Knowledge does not equal power. Knowledge plus action equals power." – **John Antonios**

"Life shrinks or expands in proportion to one's courage." – **Anais Nin**

"Success is the progressive realization of worthwhile, predetermined, personal goals." – **Paul J. Meyer**

"The mind is a powerful force. It can enslave us or empower us. Learn to use it wisely." – **Brian Tracy**

"Always bear in mind that our own resolution to succeed is more important than any other one thing." – **Abraham Lincoln**

"Well done is better than well said." – **Benjamin Franklin**

"It's not that I'm so smart; it's just that I stay with problems longer." – **Albert Einstein**

"The only real voyage of discovery consists not in seeking new landscapes but in having new eyes." – **Marcel Proust**

"The secret of success is consistency of purpose." – **Benjamin Disraeli**

"If you enjoy what you do, don't be afraid of expressing your enthusiasm. Enjoyment is infectious." – **Alan Sugar**

What words of wisdom get you motivated for a great day every morning? Let me know . . . @TomMallens #8AMINSPIRATION

Building up likability by leveraging brand you!

If people like you, they will be more likely to do business with you. As we've seen, people can't like you unless they know you.

So now that you've contacted them using Linkedin, you need to give them something to like – or not like!

Being liked on Linkedin is about the information that you share, publish and discuss together with how you engage and interact with your contacts.

The surest way to avoid being liked by anyone you're connected to on Linkedin is to do nothing.

Sadly this is an option taken by some salespeople who then complain that social media and social selling doesn't work.

It's the same logic that sees people go to networking events, stand quietly in the corner and then complain that they didn't get any useful contacts or leads from it.

Whether it's social media or face-to-face engagement, you have to actually DO something to get results.

And in that sense, doing something... anything, in fact... is better than doing nothing.

Now that you've built an audience on Linkedin, it's time to talk with them in a style that's consistent with your personal brand.

As we mentioned, this personal brand is defined by how you want people to feel when they think about you.

And it's by sharing updates that reflect this personal brand that you will build up likability.

Broadly speaking, anything you share on Linkedin can be put into one of three categories.

- Information, facts and figures (that your audience will find useful)
- Details of how to do things (that your audience want to do)
- Entertaining and sociable content (that your audience will enjoy)

If you're going to share only one type of thing on Linkedin, make it the last one.

Why? Because that is, in itself, the essence of social selling; building relationships, attracting leads and making sales through your personal brand.

Or, in other words, leveraging the power of being liked.

It's probably a good idea to share some information that your audience will find useful and explain how to do things that your audience want to do too.

But if you only share these things on Linkedin (and there are plenty of people who ONLY share those things) you will miss out on the big benefits of you leveraging your personal brand.

You will completely miss out on the power of personal connections with potential customers.

And this is kind of a shame.

Whoever you are and whatever you do in B2B sales, there will be people in your industry who will want to do business with you on the basis not just of your compelling offer and guarantee but on the basis of your shared interests, common goals and mutual ideas.

Sharing these on Linkedin is a great way to add even more power to your existing marketing assets.

On every major social media platform, you can build up likability with your contacts in some of the following ways:

- Messaging individuals directly and privately
- Publishing updates for everyone to see
- Sending messages to sub-sections of your network only
- Listening and learning about others

If you're going to do only one thing on social media, (again) make it the last one.

Just as the best sales people listen first, ask questions and then talk when they're face-to-face or on the phone with a prospect.

They do the same when they're on Linkedin.

Linkedin contains a HUGE amount of information on your potential customers that you can use to your advantage in building rapport (both online and offline).

You can see what information your potential customers publish as well as what information they have listed in their profiles that could help you when you pick up the phone and speak to them or their company.

Next, you'll need to get into the habit of regularly sharing updates with your network in one of the three other ways (private messages, public updates and messages to sub-sections of your network).

Building trust with potential customers

Finally, being trusted is about sharing and building likability consistently. But more than this, it's about making interacting with existing and potential customers on a social level a key part of your strategy.

People are almost helpless against the power of a good story to persuade and influence them.

And social media is a perfect place to tell and consistently reinforce stories about yourself, and your products and services, with potential customers.

Importantly, they don't just give you the opportunity to spread awareness of that message one-to-one.

They allow you to do that on a one-to-many basis.

And if that message is part of a consistent brand identity, your social media efforts become fantastically powerful.

Your social media activity will help you attract attention and in-bound leads together with spreading awareness of who you are, what do you and the best things about.

And these in turn will help you get more warm phone calls and face-to-face appointments with the people that matter to you in business.

Some people complain that they don't have the time for Linkedin.

The truth is, they simply haven't realised the huge opportunity and made it a habit.

One of the quickest ways to make social media quicker and easier is to use your mobile phone to show the world what you're up to while you're on the go.

Essentially, all social media networks have mobile apps you can download onto your smart phone.

So wherever you go or whatever you do in business, you can share that with all of your most important contacts.

Everyone in the world has the same number of hours in the day.

The question is only how you choose to spend the time you have.

If you understand that people do business with people they know, like and trust AND that Linkedin is a powerful way to exponentially increase the number of people that know, like and trust you, you will find a way to make time.

Start with the end goal in mind

There are a few important points to consider if you're going to get results from social selling.

First, you have to have an objective. If you don't have a specific goal you want to achieve by using Linkedin in your sales or marketing, you cannot and will not achieve it.

You must be able to explain this goal in simple business terms and you MUST write it down.

There are lots of different goals and objectives you might have for using social media.

Here are a few examples:

- You want more in-bound leads from new prospects
- You want more warm (not cold) phone calls with potential customers
- You want to increase repeat purchases
- You want to increase referrals from existing customers

A quick note on getting customers from social media

Notice that the list does not say that Linkedin will help you get more customers.

The reason is that customers are the result of the number of leads you get AND the rate at which you convert them into the sales.

They are not something that you can just get without going through these two steps.

If you do use it effectively, Linkedin will get you more leads.

And given your levels of skill, a certain proportion of these leads will convert into sales.

So, all other things being equal, Linkedin will result in you getting more customers through the process of improved lead finding.

As we'll see later in this book when we come to measuring results from Linkedin, it's important to understand this distinction.

Now back to the bit about goals...

Whatever the case, social media can help you achieve your goals but only if you can articulate what you're trying to achieve in clear and simple terms.

Let's use an example that builds on the traditional idea of a sales funnel.

In this case, it's actually a sales hourglass.

Leads come in as a result of getting a compelling offer about your products and services in front of the right people with a reason to take action.

In other words, you become known, liked and trusted by the right people.

Once you've established trust, there's a quick and easy way for people to try your product or service.

It should be something that takes the guess-work out and gives them a clear indication of what it would be like to do business with you.

It could be a free offer or a no-obligation deal of some kind.

In either case, it should lead potential customers smoothly into the buy phase.

Most people stop thinking about the sales process at this point.

The sale is made, and the job is done, right?

Wrong.

It's a sales hourglass we're talking about here and there are two more stages: Repeat and refer.

These are arguably the best stages of the sales hourglass because they're the ones where costs tend to be lower and profit margins higher.

Once you've made a sale, repeat business comes in more easily. You've done the hard work and you can focus on helping the customer keep buying rather than the hard graft of persuading them to buy in the first place.

The idea is summed up in the phrase: Most people get a customer to make a sale but smart people make a sale to get a customer.

Once someone is buying from you, it becomes MUCH easier for them to buy other products and services from you – particularly if you have a range of items that compliment the initial purchase well.

So, just as you can use social media to increase the number of people who know you, like you and trust you, you can use social media to increase the number of people who buy a second, third or fourth time from you AND the number of people who then refer you on to friends, colleagues and suitable contacts.

Socialising with people and introducing an incentive to refer you can be your objective from the outset.

The key is deciding which of these different goals is the most important to your business.

If you can concentrate on achieving one specific goal for attracting or retaining customers, you will be more successful than if you try to do all 7 stages at once.

You don't have to perfect every stage before you move on to the next one but start with an objective to improve one area and then introduce similar objectives in other areas of the sales hourglass.

Leads in here

5 minutes of planning is worth 50 minutes of doing!

Once you've identified the key business objectives you want to achieve and how Linkedin can help, you can start to think about what you can do in practice.

I've found one of the best ways to get this right is to take a quick step backwards and look at your marketing and sales as a whole.

Just 5 minutes spent thinking about your marketing and how Linkedin will fit in will make a HUGE difference further down the line.

You see, most people get super-charged on enthusiasm like a teenage kid discovering cider for the first time and jump onto social media.

They make a lot of noise and are very busy for a day, week or month but it doesn't actually achieve anything.

Just as in the case with the sales hourglass, it's because they don't have a plan.

I hate long, over-complicated plans but a 5-minute plan is sometimes all you need.

Decide what you want to achieve, think about how you can achieve it best, then write it down and start doing.

You can always change your approach later based on the feedback from your initial steps.

Writing your plans, objectives and goals down is CRUCIAL!

Without writing them down, they remain forever stuck in the realm of your thoughts.

Write them down and your thoughts (both figuratively and literally) take the first step to becoming real things; real achievements in the real world rather than ideas in your head.

They are now ideas made into a real, tangible item – albeit a paper-thin one.

If you've got 10 minutes, then do the following excellent exercise.

Think about your marketing as a pyramid.

The most fundamentally important aspects are at the bottom. If the base of your pyramid isn't secure, the whole thing will fall down later.

In this case, the foundation of all your marketing must be your brand.

Your brand is the intangible emotions you want people to associate with you and your products and services.

It's how you want them to feel. It's the experience of working with you.

Try to define this in terms of adjectives. Is your brand funky, sexy and crazy? Or is it slick, refined and debonair?

Once you have clear emotions you want your brand to evoke, you must reinforce them EVERY time you engage with the customer.

In many senses, this emotion you evoke is actually more important than your product itself.

In fact, your physical product or service is NOT your product at all.

The feeling people get when they buy is the true product you're selling.

Any physical assets you exchange when a sale is made are just ways to help transfer this emotion onto the customer.

If you buy a new car for £110,995 it will not (legally at least) get you to your destination faster than a car that costs £11,995 new.

The reason people pay the extra £100,000 for a car is because they want to feel a certain way about themselves or they want others to feel a certain way about them when they find out they have that type of car.

Specifically, they want to feel successful and be associated with pleasant feelings of high status, achievement and luxury.

But these are just feelings. The car itself is not the product. The feelings are what people are buying.

If you're a micro-business, it's very easy to decide on the right brand identity of your business because (all other things being equal) it will probably be a reflection of you and your unique personality.

Defining this brand in clear terms is important for two reasons:

1. Because it underpins all your marketing activity. Every bit of your marketing should consistently convey the same emotions in the minds of customers and potential customers.

2. People only make buying decisions based on emotion. Even people who think they buy purely on logic only think that way because, ultimately, they're the kind of people who like to feel like they make logical decisions.

For these reasons, clearly defining the emotions you want your brand to be associated with is essential for success on Linkedin.

It informs everything from the platforms you use to the words you use when you update you or your company's status.

Be warned, saying you want your brand to be about 'excellent customer service' is missing the point.

Excellent customer service is not an emotion.

You can have excellent customer service delivered in a serious and sombre way like the service at a funeral directors or in a cosy, homely and warm manner like going to your grandmother's house as a child; there's a big difference!

Only once you've defined your brand in emotional terms can you think about the rest of your marketing activity.

In particular, your specific businesses offering, the marketing infrastructure it uses to deliver that offer, the content it uses to help people try before they buy and the way in which it socializes with potential customers – either face-to-face or on social media platforms.

Your socialising and social media

Your content

Your infastructure

Your offers

Your brand
What emotions do you want to define your brand?

If an 8 year old can't understand it, it's too complicated

As shown in the marketing pyramid diagram, your offers are built on the foundation of your brand.

You must be able to sum up your offers quickly and concisely whether it's verbally or in a social media update.

If you can't explain what you do in terms an 8-year-old can understand, it's not simple enough and you'll never be able to get what you do across in the quick and simply way that Linkedin demands.

One of the big reasons people don't give referrals or pass your details on to people you know that might need your products and services is because they don't actually understand what you do.

Sure, they might know roughly what you do – "something to do with electronics", "some type of chemicals for the oil and gas industry", or "a kind of domain names for the internet type thing," – but very often they don't know exactly.

If people can't explain what you do when you've met them face-to-face, how on earth will they understand if you can't sum it up in short, clear and concise terminology on social media.

Offers NOT offer

If you're wondering why it says offers with an 'S' at the end, it's because ideally, you should have different offers for different target markets.

Your offer for customers in the medical textiles sector may be very different than your offer for customers in industrial upholstery – even though the product you're selling may be very similar or completely identical.

It needs to be presented in a different way and may have completely different marketing material associated with it.

When it comes to Linkedin, you may want to target some messages to different audiences and write them in a different way, as a result.

All of the main social media platforms offer a way to categorise people you're connected to so that you can send messages tailored to their particular characteristics.

So you can encourage them to visit different websites tailored to their particular needs, rather than generic websites trying to cater for everyone.

As you build rapport with new contacts on Linkedin, you can encourage them to visit useful websites that will contain useful information for them.

Crucially, these websites can be tailored specifically to their needs.

Good business is built on good infrastructure

Next up in the marketing pyramid, your infrastructure is the means – or medium – by which you deliver your offer to potential customers.

That means it includes your business cards, website, brochures, leaflets, direct mail letters, email footers and promotional gifts; in fact anything you use to communicate with your customers that isn't the words coming out of your mouth.

You might have scores of different channels to deliver your message or just a carefully-selected handful.

If you have just one way of getting your message to market, you probably have some problems brewing very shortly.

Notice that the infrastructure is the third tier of the marketing triangle.

You must not decide you're going to promote your business on Linkedin and then worry about what you're going to say.

You should first establish you brand, then develop your offers for particular target markets and THEN, and only then, decide what is the best infrastructure to help you do that.

You want to be where your target customers are but if you haven't carefully defined your target customers, how can you know where they are online and which social media platforms they're most likely to be on?

Content – like cash – is king!

If people know, like and trust you enough to start checking out your marketing material, they might be interested in actually trying your products and services.

So make it easy for them with some great content.

Content is your way of letting potential customers try before they buy and giving them a flavour of what it would be like to work with you or buy from you.

It could be a blog where you share great tips and information.

It could be a podcast, video or images that show how your business operates and conveys its unique style.

Whatever it is, it must be consistent with your brand and must help strengthen the relationship between you and your potential customer.

In particular, it must de-mystify the buying process.

One big reason people don't buy is fear. Fear that they will buy the wrong product and realise they have made a costly mistake afterwards (when it's already too late).

Content is a way to placate these fears by letting customers road test you.

That means giving them an appropriate way to see exactly what would be involved in buying.

How is your service delivered? What does the customer have to do? How long will it take?

Will you have to visit their office several times? Will they have to come to you? How long will the meetings take? Are there any hidden costs involved? What people will they have to speak with to move the process forward?

Anything you can do to clarify this with content that helps people try before they buy will directly benefit your sales efforts.

Finally, now you've got all that in place, you can think about adding a purely social element to your marketing.

Socialising is, was and always will be one of the prime ways that business gets done.

Just ask any businessman why they play golf. They're often not actually huge golf fans.

They do it because it's a chance to socialise with prospects, leads and referral partners.

Whether it's face-to-face socialising through networking and corporate hospitality or online socialising through social media, how you interact and socialise with people must, once again, be consistent with your brand.

Get this link between your brand and your social media right and that's where the lead-finding, word-of-mouth marketing and referral magic happens.

Get it wrong and you just spend a lot of time making a lot of noise on Linkedin, Twitter and Facebook.

But that noise isn't actually achieving anything. And I'm sure you've got better things to be doing with your time.

Imagine going to an industry business event and talking non-stop with people about football and last night's new TV drama.

It's lots of fun but if you NEVER introduce an invitation to follow-up, continue the conversation or buy from you directly, you're just socialising for socialising's sake, which is doubtless lots of fun but not very productive in a business sense.

By now, you hopefully have a much clearer idea of how Linkedin can help you to achieve your sales objectives, together with some valuable information about the difference between a traditional sales approach to lead-finding and a social sales approach.

In the next section of the book, we're going to look more closely at Linkedin specifically.

And I'll explain why I believe it's the BEST and quickest social media platform for the pro-active sales professional.

The good news is that reading this book alone is an investment in your skills that already proves you're among the most pro-active people out there – and that alone is a great indication that you're set for success.

So far, we've gone through a quick overview of leads and the thinking behind social media.

So now we've got all that cleared up. It's time to get down to business...

MORNING MOTIVATION

"Good business people aren't so through what they know, but because of an insatiable need to know more." – **Michael E. Gerber**

"Success is to be measured not so much by the position that one has reached in life as by the obstacles which he has overcome."
– **Booker T. Washington**

"All the adversity in my life strengthened me. A kick in the teeth may be the best thing for you." – **Walt Disney**

"A person who never made a mistake never tried anything new."
– **Albert Einstein**

"Even if you fall on your face, you're still moving forward."
– **Victor Kiam**

"Why not go out on a limb? Isn't that where the fruit is?"
– **Frank Scully**

"If something is important enough you should try, even if the probable outcome is failure." – **Elon Musk**

"You become what you believe." – **Oprah Winfrey**

"Life is too short to have a bad day. You have a bad half hour, then move on." – **Brad Sugars**

"It is never too late to be what you might have been." – **George Eliot**

What words of wisdom get you motivated for a great day every morning? Let me know . . . @TomMallens #8AMINSPIRATION

HAVE YOU SEEN THIS WOMAN?

Tracy Jones is wanted for social sales training. Tracy is 42 years old. She is marketing manager at an IT company in Reading. Tracy could help her company get more leads more easily and more often if they spent just 3.5 hours learning how to use Linkedin in an effective way, without making the mistakes most sales and marketing people make that stop them getting a steady stream of leads and referrals.

Call +44 (0)1926 678 920 NOW to help Tracey master social sales and get more leads!

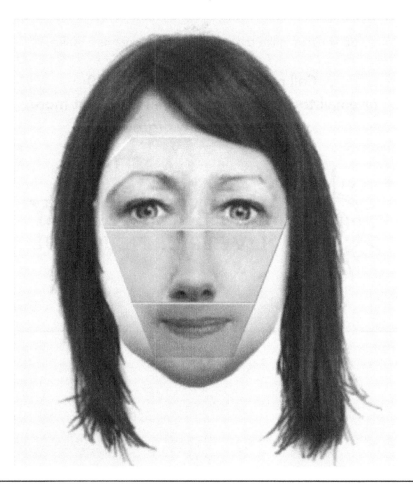

DO YOU WANT TO BE THE BEST YOU CAN BE?

Not just in work?

But in life too?

42% of men say their biggest fear is not achieving their dreams.

In my spare time, I run men's self-development mastermind network Mentality.

We help you achieve your goals – whether they are work-related or not.

So you can make the epic life of your dreams a reality.

**Call me on +44(0)1926 678 920
or email tom@tommallens.com to find out more.
www.iammentality.org/events**

MENTALITY
LIVE EPIC. DIE JOYFUL.

CHAPTER 1

The amazing opportunity at your finger tips

WHAT WORKS BEST FOR YOU IN SALES?

Do you have hints or tips that help you beat gatekeepers?

Or specific questions about anything in this book?

Drop me a line on Linkedin or Twitter

And I'll do my best to answer!

www.linkedin.com/in/TomMallens
@TomMallens #GetPastTheGatekeeper

When you're in a regular job and dream of working for yourself, you almost inevitably bump into the Steve Jobs and Richard Bransons of this world in online articles telling you to 'just do it'.

To quit the job and go after your dream.

It's hard to stay focused on work when there's another article on Harvard Business Review.org promising to tell you The 7 Traits You MUST Have to Make it in Business or The 5 Qualities of Every Successful Entrepreneur.

Wow. If you just know the names of those special super-power abilities, you'll be set to take over the world with your incredible business idea.

Customers and sales will start to pour into your business and you'll be sitting on a global empire like Bill Gates in no time.

You're full of enthusiasm. You're going to pick up the phone, get calling and then sales and loads of money will inevitably be yours.

Unfortunately, life generally has other plans.

In my case, I found myself sat in my sister's freezing cold basement squeezing myself up against the barely-functioning radiator wondering why the manufacturing sector's army of receptionists didn't realise that my call to their switchboard was the most important one of their boss's working week.

After leaving life as editor of a national trade magazine, I decided to go to business school for a year.

It was a fantastic year in which 160 students from around the world had their heads pumped full of statistical models, finance equations and management psychology in a bid to turn them into the CEOs of global mega-corporations.

Knowing only that I wanted to go and work abroad or work for myself (or possibly both) after graduating, opportunity thrust itself upon me when my dad got made redundant after years of excellent service at a large plastics company.

Never one to take things lying down, he offered to take the redundancy but carry on working for them as a salesman on a commission-only basis.

It was a win-win for both parties.

After a few years on his own, my dad hit retirement and decided to take a well-deserved rest to work on his golf and wine-tasting skills.

It was my opportunity to work for myself for the first time.

I would become the greatest manufacturing sector salesman in history and the sales and money would pour in effortlessly.

I decided to collaborate with my sister who would handle the day-to-day admin while I convinced companies to spend hundreds of thousands of pounds on machinery and specialist raw material plastics.

We established an agreement with another company in the composites sector to give us a more stable financial base than the plastics company alone and got to work building our empire.

These big ambitions were quickly met with a harsh dose of reality.

No-one in the manufacturing sector knew who I was. And no-one cared.

I'll never forget my dad's explanation for why he didn't have any business cards.

"Everyone who needs to know me already does," he explained.

My dad was known in the industry. After years spent building contacts at exhibitions and face-to-face meetings, he either knew most of the potential customers out there directly. Or he knew someone that did.

I, on the other-hand, did not.

Which meant that as far as most prospective customers were concerned, I was not worth speaking to.

My cold calls were going badly. Really badly.

Most of them ended in me being invited to "send some information in" to a dustbin the company in question had recently installed.

After months of this, my motivation levels were at an all-time low.

It was around this time that I got the opportunity to go to a manufacturing sector exhibition in Paris.

It was three days of companies who couldn't possibly reject my calls when I was stood directly in front of them.

Amid the over-priced sandwiches and organised chaos of the exhibition, I got talking to a fellow salesman who mentioned he'd got some leads for machinery sales from Linkedin.

This was news to me. Back at business school, Linkedin was presented as the ultimate job-hunting tool for people looking to shin their way up the greasy pole of corporate management.

It was NEVER discussed as a tool for finding leads in the B2B sales sector.

With my appetite and enthusiasm for cold calling at an all-time low, I resolved to pour my energy into scouring Linkedin for leads, chances to call prospects who actually wanted to speak to me, and opportunities to move our sales business forward.

I searched Linkedin for every technical director, purchasing manager and boss of a manufacturing company I could find.

I used my profile to explain all the great benefits our products would bring.

And I created and published some free guides about changes in different parts of the manufacturing industry that presented lucrative opportunities for our potential customers.

Finally, and importantly, I used it regularly. Not logging in once a week to read more of those Become-a-Millionaire-in-5-Minutes-a-Week articles.

But proactively hunting out opportunities to contact the types of people I knew could potentially benefit from our machinery and raw materials.

I was always looking for opportunities to make contact with people so that when I called they believed it was worth giving me 5 minutes of their time.

I quickly got the kinds of results that convinced me this time on Linkedin was time well spent.

I found the names of all the technical staff at an aerospace company in Wales – one whose reception had turned away my previous cold calls.

I did some super-fast research on them and discovered from Linkedin that one of them was having technical difficulties with a manufacturing process our machinery could potentially solve.

With a clear customer need and a few messages on my side, my subsequent phone calls went straight through to the right people.

Rapport and trust was established and before I knew it, I was invited to a tour of their production facility.

This time, no receptionist could stop me. Successful sales appointments were finally within my grasp.

It was around this time that I was discussing some changes in the aerospace seating sector that created a BIG opportunity for the range of industrial flatbed laminating equipment we sold.

So with Linkedin a big focus of my efforts, I created a short guide to this opportunity and decided to publicise it to as many people in the UK aerospace sector as I could.

It was nothing fancy. A Word document with a few pictures converted into a PDF and uploaded to various discussion groups on Linkedin.

The kinds of places the people that might buy our machinery would go to talk about their businesses online.

I uploaded it and hoped to get a few enquiries from people wanting to know more.

Perhaps, I'd get some warm phone calls that I could convert into face-to-face appointments.

Instead, about 2 weeks later, I got an email from a guy called George, the head of an aerospace research institute in Ireland.

He'd been passed the guide I'd created by a colleague who saw it on Linkedin.

He was organising a conference in a few months' time in Germany for 32 of Europe's biggest players in automotive and aerospace seating.

And having seen from the guide that I (apparently) knew what I was talking about, he invited me to be a key-note speaker.

This was exactly the kind of opportunity we needed to catapult awareness of our machinery to the next level.

It was then that I understood how simple it was.

George had got in contact with me because he knew I existed, he liked and valued the content I'd produced and, based on a look at my Linkedin profile, trusted that I'd do a good job.

Simply knowing about the (completely inanimate) machinery we sold wasn't enough.

He had to like and trust me, a person, to get in touch and offer me the opportunity.

So, I figured, the more people in relevant manufacturing sectors I can get to know, like and trust me, the better.

Who knows what kinds of opportunities I could then start to tap into.

In the absence of already being known by all the right people in the sector (like my dad), Linkedin could help me build just enough rapport with people to make that transition from a stranger trying to sell them stuff they didn't want to a trustworthy contact who it was worth having a chat to.

It was as simple as being known, liked and trusted by as many of the right kinds of people in the industry as possible.

That's what would get me those initial leads, calls and opportunities to move our business forward.

Over the coming chapters, we'll look at how you can become better known, liked and trusted by the key people in your industry more easily using Linkedin.

On the way, we'll drop in on some social science research from Harvard, a boxing match and lots of practical tips you can benefit from immediately.

But more of that later. Right now, it's time to look at how you can become better known by the key decision makers in your industry and why it's important.

CHAPTER 2

Why it pays to be better known

WANT AN EASIER LIFE?

Would it make your life easier if your sales team was bringing in more business?

My training courses and conference speeches show your sales team exactly how to do just that.

In three easy steps!

Which means they get the know-how they need to become masters of social selling with Linkedin.

And you get a sales team that's getting more in-bound sales leads, more warm phone calls (rather than awkward cold ones) and more business opportunities.

Just check out the testimonials on page 251 to see what some of my recent customers like you think.

Then drop me a message on tom@tommallens.com or a call on +44(0)1926 678 920 to find out how your team could get more leads too.

f one of your friends needed a favour, you'd do your best to try and help them, right?

Sure. That's what friends do. You help each other out in your personal lives and if they ask, in business too.

In the workplace, you might send them useful information; get them access to key people; connect them with valuable opportunities . . . the list goes on.

On the other hand, if a total stranger calls and asks for help in their career, most people are less likely to offer assistance.

You don't know them. You don't know why they've got in touch. You're unsure of their motives.

The situation is unpredictable and your brain is full of concerns, worries and suspicions.

In most cases, most people politely decline to help out people they've never met.

But what about the people in between those two extremes. People that aren't your friends and yet aren't strangers either?

What about your acquaintances and people that know someone you know?

These could be colleagues from different departments or casual acquaintances from a sports club.

The kind of person you bump into once every couple of months; make small talk with and then carry on with your day.

Harvard, and later Stanford, University sociologist Mark Granovetter called these people 'weak ties' – as oppose to your good friends and close business contacts who are your 'strong ties'.

During a seminal study of how 282 top business executives got their current jobs, Granovetter proved what most people intuitively know.

That people will gladly help their friends when they ask for help looking for a job.

He also showed that people approached by strangers asking for help to get a new job will usually politely decline to assist.

However, Granovetter proved that close friends are not necessarily the best source of new opportunities.

In fact, weak ties are a better source of new opportunities, referrals and introductions than people you know extremely well.

The reason why is extremely important to anyone who takes networking, social media or relationship building seriously.

Weak ties give people access to social groups they don't normally mix with or belong to.

In fact, most people hear about job or other business opportunities from weak ties.

We talk to our close friends all the time. We work along side them and read the same books, blogs and newspapers.

By the time they've heard of possible new opportunities, we probably know about them as well.

Weak ties on the other hand, tell us about opportunities we'd normally never otherwise hear about.

So the larger your pool of weak ties, the bigger the stream of new ideas, opportunities and business possibilities that will start to flow your way.

The bigger your network of peripheral contacts who you know 'a bit', the better.

As Granovetter himself explained: "Individuals with few weak ties will be deprived of information from distant parts of the social system and will be confined to the provincial news and views of their close friends.

"This deprivation will not only insulate them from the latest ideas and fashions but may put them at a disadvantaged position in the labour market where advancement can depend on knowing about openings at just the right time."

Social media – and Linkedin in particular – is a fantastic place to build a huge community of weak ties; people who know you a bit and are in contact with you every so often.

One of the best reasons for this is because Linkedin acts as a contacts map; telling you not only who you know but VERY importantly, who they also know.

Linkedin calls these people '2nd connections'. Granovetter, who was most recently the Joan Butler Ford Professor in the School of Humanities and Sciences at Stanford, would call them 'weak ties'.

On average, most people have between 300 and 500 connections on Linkedin.

So every time you bring a new 'strong' and trusted connection into your network, there are 300 to 500 new connections who are just one referral away in their 2nd line network.

I remember putting this theory to the test. Back then my Linkedin network was 1,146 connections strong.

And off the back, I had 509,333 2nd line connections.

That's more than half a million people who were potentially just one introduction away from me.

If you have a network of even a couple of hundred contacts, you will find there are thousands of people you can potentially get introductions to.

Go on, try it now and find out.

Mentioning the fact that you have a connection in common is just one of the great ways to build rapport and bring new Linkedin members into your network.

Alternatively, you can find people in your 2nd line network who you think are potential customers and ask for introductions to them from your best 'strong tie' connections – that is, the people you know best in your 1st line network.

The key thing to remember is that for weak ties to be useful, you still have to be in contact with them.

Not every day, not every week and not every month but OCCASSIONALLY!

Taking a moment to think about how often you'll communicate with your network on Linkedin will help you keep in contact with your weak ties more easily.

And as Mark Granovetter proved, that's a great thing for business!

Building and keeping in contact with a network of people who know, like and trust you is vital.

As billionaire businessman Robert Kiyosaki said: "Successful people look to build networks. Everyone else looks for work."

Most people in sales will consciously (or unconsciously) do this already.

But too many people miss out by failing to build a strong online community too.

By building and keeping in contact with a network of Linkedin contacts, you are tending to your strong ties AND building a huge pool of weak ties that you can dip in to for new opportunities, ideas and introductions.

If you're not using social media to proactively manage your professional network, showcase your expertise as the go-to person in your field, and add-value to the people that know you, you're missing out on all the great business opportunities that follow.

So always be building your networks on social media and increasing the number of people that know, like and trust you.

And you don't have to take my word for it. It's proper science 'guv. Just ask Mark Granovetter.

This brings us onto a second and related point.

If you're going to sell anything and get people coming to you with enquiries, there is one thing you MUST do above all other things.

You must be talked about.

That's right, it is essential in sales that you are being talked about.

Think about it, if people are not talking about you, you quite literally cannot sell anything.

This starts at the most simple level of someone talking about you to themselves; thinking about you and listening to that voice in their heads that convinces themselves that it's a good idea to listen to what you have to say or to give you that chance to speak to them on the phone.

And it extends all the way up to you being name-dropped into conversations by the great and the good within your sector at exhibitions, events, in the trade press and in private conversations.

In fact, I'll go so far as to say that the more you are talked about the better – regardless of what they're saying about you.

If you're the one being discussed, opportunities and openings for business naturally flow as a result.

At its most fundamental level, that's the phenomenon with modern celebrities.

They're no longer people who have achieved anything significant.

They're simply people who are talked about a lot (in newspapers, gossip magazines, chat shows, pubs, Facebook discussions and internet forums).

Whether you're into celebrity gossip culture or not, the point is that being talked about in and of itself creates interesting and potentially lucrative opportunities.

If you can combine that with some substance, value and a compelling offer for a product or service that people in your industry will value, it starts to become a powerful tool in your social sales arsenal.

So what do you have to do to get talked about?

Here is the answer (brace yourself because it might shock you).

First of all you have to do . . .

Something.

In fact, to start with you just have to do anything.

Yes, that's right, anything that will get the attention of people and stand out from the ordinary.

Do something that catches people's attention and you will start to be remembered and be talked about more often.

And when your name is being thrown around (and people remember what you do and how you help people), opportunities begin to follow –

especially when you make it easy for people to find and get in contact with you by being ever-present on social media.

The US thinker, strategist and author Seth Godin called this the Purple Cow strategy.

Everyone knows cows are (without getting into a discussion about the many different breeds – let's assume we're talking about friesians here) black and white.

So no-one talks to their friends or business contacts about the fact that they saw a black and white cow.

It's normal, forgettable and boring.

A purple cow on the other hand. Now that's interesting, unusual and different.

Exactly the kind of thing people will mention to other people within your industry.

Being different, memorable and unique is vital to being talked about.

And being talked about is vital to spreading awareness of who you are and what you do (both on an individual and company level).

Social media platforms like Linkedin become the rocket fuel that you can pour onto your sales and marketing activities; helping to spread awareness of who you are and what you do within the key decision makers in your sector.

It's a great approach to take from a career point of view too because, the more unique you are, the more difficult it becomes to replace you.

Think about it for a second. If you are like everyone else, joining the dots of your day-to-day sales processes with robotic precision, sooner or later, your employer will realise they can simply get a robot to replace you.

There is nothing you do that someone else can't for less money.

But stand out with a unique, vibrant and unforgettable quality, personality or skill and no-one else will be able to imitate what you do.

You will become irreplaceable.

I was at a composites industry awards dinner once when I met a salesman for a well-known company in the UK carbon fibre composites industry.

He was irrepressibly energetic and had a huge beard; the kind that the uber-trendy hipsters of London would be proud of.

No-one I saw speak to him could resist making a joke or comment about it.

It didn't surprise me to learn he was one of the company's top-performing sales people largely because people in the industry remembered exactly who he was and what products he offered.

They talked about him and mentioned his name a lot in conversation with other people.

Which meant he was always at the centre of the grapevine when new opportunities and ideas were making their way through the industry.

I'm not suggesting for a moment that having a beard makes you a better salesperson.

But I am suggesting that being different, standing out and being talked about within your industry as a result helps you hear of more new opportunities for business than being the same as everyone else and not being talked about does.

If you rely on word-of-mouth alone to spread this awareness of how interesting and different you are, you'll get results.

But that information will spread MUCH more rapidly, widely and effectively if you're using social media to supercharge it too.

And if you work in the manufacturing, technology or IT industries, or any other B2B sales sector, Linkedin is by far the best social media platform to use to help you achieve this.

MORNING MOTIVATION

"Great people create their lives. Everyone else waits to see where life takes them next." – **Michael E. Gerber**

"The path to success is to take massive, determined action."
– **Anthony Robbins**

"Live as if you were to die tomorrow. Learn as if you were to live to forever." – **Mahatma Gandhi**

"We are what we repeatedly do. Excellence then is not an act but a habit." – **Aristotle**

"Believe you can and you're halfway there." – **Theodore Roosevelt**

"I never worry about the problem. I worry about the solution."
– **Shaquille O'Neal**

"Start where you are. Use what you have. Do what you can."
– **Arthur Ashe**

"Our business in life is not to get ahead of others, but to get ahead of ourselves." – **Zig Ziglar**

"Don't have dreams. Have things you do." – **Matt Krause**

"There are no traffic jams along the extra mile." – **Roger Staubach**

"Most fear is just bad management of our own mental faculties. Get over it!" – **Brendon Burchard**

What words of wisdom get you motivated for a great day every morning? Let me know . . . @TomMallens #8AMINSPIRATION

AN INTERESTING THOUGHT TO HELP YOU SELL MORE

If you understand how something works, it becomes easier to get good at it, right?

Which means that if you understand how sales works, it becomes easier to make more sales.

Here are 6 steps in the sales process:

1. Find and identify prospects
2. Make contact and build rapport
3. Get information
4. Check the facts
5. Make a proposal
6. Ask for the business

Linkedin can help a LOT with the first three steps in this sales process.

I can also help you get better at the other three too.

If you'd like to know exactly how Linkedin can help you make more sales, just drop me a line.

Don't worry, I won't try any high-pressure sales stuff.

It's a quick chat and if it's not right for you, it's zero problem.

But you don't know unless you ask.

So give me a quick call on +44(0)1926 678 920 or email tom@tommallens.com.

CHAPTER 3

How you can become better known by prospects

#GetPastTheGatekeeper

S o, you want to start building and maintaining a powerful network of contacts on Linkedin to help in your B2B sales efforts, right?

But steady on there a second! Don't go all Usain Bolt on me and dash off towards the finish line just yet.

If you ask yourself the three following questions, you'll be MUCH better placed to start getting great results. So here they are . . .

1. What do you actually want to achieve on Linkedin?

One of the biggest mistakes people make is not having an idea of why they use Linkedin.

Ask yourself what your ideal outcome is. It might simply be getting the names of key people in a target company or sector.

It might be building rapport and getting in-bound leads from new potential customers.

It might be reducing churn in your customer base by engaging existing customers to help keep them for longer.

Whatever you want to achieve, knowing what it is, is vital to being able to achieve it.

So take a moment to think about what you're trying to achieve in top-line business terms.

And translate that into an objective on Linkedin and B2B social media.

2. What types of people do you want to contact?

Now you know your objective, who are the types of people you want to build relationships with on Linkedin?

Linkedin offers incredible search functions that allow you to pinpoint specific people and build relationships with them.

As soon as you know who you want to speak to, you can start to find them, then build up likeability and trust over time.

3. Why would someone want to talk to you?

However painful it is to hear, no-one is actually interested in speaking to you on Linkedin unless you give them a reason!

Without getting into a long and tedious debate about it, it's human nature.

People don't want to speak to other people unless there's something in it for them.

It's so easy to forget and it's one of the reasons many people fail at social media.

Remember, that the clue is in the name. It's called 'social' media because it's most effective when you use it to socialise with other people.

Many people forget that however awesome and amazing they think they are, they still have to write their marketing copy with the customer – and not themselves – in mind.

But before you get depressed about the fact that no-one wants to speak to you, the good news is that what other people really DO want is solutions to their problems (whatever those problems might be).

Understanding what value you can offer other people in the Linkedin community to help them solve their problems is crucial to starting conversations and getting great results.

It might be a free guide. It might be a free consultation session. It could be introductions to influential people. It could just be the offer to help out.

Whatever it is, understand your value to others and communicate it. If you can use your value to help others, Linkedin quickly becomes a key part of your sales and marketing that really helps drive your business forward.

Building your network

So now you're ready to start building your network with a clear idea of what you want to achieve. Well done!

But where do you get your Linkedin connections from? The answer is probably, quite literally, right in front of you.

Inviting colleagues, existing customers, potential customers and professional contacts to connect with you on Linkedin is a great place to start.

Most people know hundreds – and usually thousands – of other people in business.

This means you're already sat on a goldmine of opportunities they're not fully taking advantage of.

From the person sat next to you at work, networkers at the local business breakfast club, to the potential customers you met at a recent trade exhibition.

Building your network with the people you already know is the easiest place to start.

To really make this work for you, it's not enough to simply ask people to connect.

In today's information-overloaded world, you have to give them a reason.

What benefit will they get by connecting to you?

If there's no benefit, the chances of them doing it are somewhere between low and very low.

Make this benefit clear in all your marketing material and you'll find a steady stream of new connections quickly accumulates.

The benefit of connecting to me on Linkedin is that I'll give you time-effective tips on getting more leads from Linkedin in 3 easy steps.

If you can be equally as clear on the benefits of joining your network on Linkedin, you send out a clear and consistent message that quickly spreads both online and off about who you are and why you're a useful person to know.

Repeat this message across ALL your marketing material:

- Business cards
- Email footers
- Websites
- Brochures
- Headed paper
- And anything else you can think of . . .

Connecting with the people you know is important. But there's more.

Something that's even closer to home than the colleague sat opposite you.

In fact, it's possibly in the desk you sit at everyday.

Business cards might seem old-fashioned in an age of digital technology but most people have hundreds of them gathering dust in a drawer at work.

And each one represents a potential business opportunity.

Ask yourself this: Would you find it weird if someone you met 3 years ago phoned up out of the blue and asked for a favour? Probably!

In the same way, many of the people in that pile of business cards in your desk might be very useful business contacts.

But you can't just ring them up out of the blue. Most people would consider it a bit weird.

Re-connecting with people on Linkedin is a great way to re-warm relationships in a 'softly softly' way.

Just be honest about it. Find them on Linkedin and send them a message: "Hi Hakim, I was just going through some old business cards and I remembered meeting you 2 years ago at the veterinary conference. I'm running a surgery in Glasgow now. It would be good to keep in touch on Linkedin."

Between the people you know now and the people you've met over your career so far, this is a great way to quickly build a large network of contacts and get back in touch with useful connections in a polite and unobtrusive manner.

STAY SOCIAL

Your mobile phone is one of the best ways to keep in contact with your key contacts through social media mobile apps.

Don't leave home without it.

Let me know where you are while you're reading this on Linkedin or Twitter.

@TomMallens

The advanced search

Once you've built your network with people you already know AND people you used to know and want to get back in touch with, it's time to turn to Linkedin itself to keep building your network.

The advanced search feature is fantastic for this.

The standard (i.e. free) Linkedin account allows you to search for potential customers on the basis of 8 key criteria. These are:

Keywords - Words listed in the person's profile. Don't forget to put this in quote marks if it's more than 1 word.

First name - Probably not relevant if you're looking for general prospects.

Last name - As above.

Title - Meaning a person's job title. For example: purchasing manager. Don't forget to put this in quote marks if it's more than 1 word.

Company - This is a great option if you're targeting large corporations with a big workforce.

School - A great option for getting in touch with specific people that used to go to the same school as you but may not be relevant here.

Postcode - A great option if your ideal customer is based within a certain distance to you.

Relationship - In most cases you'll want to tick the 2nd connections button. 2nd connections are people connected to someone you're connected to on Linkedin – even if they're not actually connected to you... yet.

Linkedin is great for salespeople who can define their potential customers or key contacts according to all or some of these 8 criteria.

The fact is, it will work less well if your target customer is 'anyone in business' or something similarly vague.

Although if your ideal customer really is 'anyone in business' you've probably got other problems related to your marketing!

Understanding Linkedin groups

Finding potential customers using the advanced search is a great way to prospect for new customers.

And so are Linkedin groups. Groups are simply sub-sections of the Linkedin community defined by common user interest.

Whatever your professional interests, there will almost certainly be a group on Linkedin where other people go to discuss the issues affecting them in business.

Groups are a great place to search for potential customers, referral partners and industry influencers.

Referral partners are people with a non-competing interest in the same types of customer.

In other words, they're people that could pass you work – it's well worth building relationships with these types of people.

Most people on Linkedin are in lots of groups.

But the majority of people don't get value - never mind leads, sales and business opportunities - because they misunderstand the value of groups and the opportunity to position themselves as an expert in their field within a chosen industry.

So how do some people become well-known influencers in Linkedin groups and translate that into real business influence?

The first step is avoiding these 3 classic mistakes of Linkedin groups.

1. Joining too many of the wrong groups

Most people have joined far too many groups packed with the wrong type of people.

In most cases, their instinct is to join groups full of people like them. In other words, their competitors!

Try to join groups full of potential customers instead.

Decide which groups will contain large numbers of your potential customers.

This includes your ideal customers, along with other useful contacts, referral partners, strategic allies and thought leaders.

Then assess which of these groups offers the demographics most valuable to you.

Once you've found the best groups, you have the opportunity to become a key influencer and an expert in your field more easily.

2. Not posting, discussing and engaging with useful contacts

As with everything in business, you have to make things happen. So ask questions, post material that's helpful to other group members, search through the group members to find the most useful business contacts and start building relationships with the RIGHT people (building contacts with the wrong people is a recipe for wasting time).

Many questions and updates in groups get ignored without attracting any discussions because people fail to ask interesting questions.

Posting a link explaining how brilliant your products and services are is NOT an interesting question.

3. Not taking your conversations offline

If you want to get the best possible results, you have to be able to take relationships with key people off-line.

No matter how good your social media, few people will send you their credit card details on Linkedin itself (although decent landing pages with a compelling offer to buy are another matter).

When the time is right, it's time to pick up the telephone and actually speak to the people you're interacting with on Linkedin – especially if they're potential customers.

You'll find the engagement on Linkedin counts for a lot when it comes to creating warm (rather than awkward and stressful cold) phone calls.

Failing to follow up with people in groups is one of the key reasons people fail to get results from Linkedin.

So be proactive and use Linkedin to build your network of existing contacts, combined with new prospects from the advanced search and groups.

All the while you'll be building the number of people that know you and laying the foundations for developing likability and trust in the future.

Don't forget that if you're going to really get to know people on Linkedin – just like in face-to-face meetings – you have to actually interact with them.

This is where a lot of people go wrong. Would you simply walk up to someone and shove your business card in their face? Probably not.

You'd actually speak to them first, right? So why not do the same on Linkedin.

Sending messages to your contacts is really important to spread awareness of who you are and what you do.

Sending the right kind of messages is crucial for generating rapport with the people you're connected to.

Because if you don't have any rapport with the people you're connected with, what's the point of being connected to them?

Here's a quick recap of the key messages to send, what to say in them, and when.

1. Connection request

If you rely on Linkedin's standard message you will struggle to generate any rapport or engagement with new contacts.

Remember, if you're using Linkedin effectively, a lot of the people you're connecting with are probably potential customers. If you're not building rapport with them, you're missing out on sales opportunities.

The standard Linkedin connection request message reads: "Hi, I'd like to add you to my professional network on Linkedin."

It hardly shows much thought or care. Would you say this to someone you'd met face-to-face? If not, then why say it online?

Filling your message full of rapport-building information is vital to getting a solid foundation for a follow-up, whether it's another message, a phone call, a request for a face-to-face meeting or something completely different.

It's a great idea to include some or all of the following in your message.

- How you met and/or found their profile (as appropriate)

- A reference to who you know that they also know (Linkedin tells you this).

- Any shared interests or activities (you can find this out from the person's profile).

- A reason why you're getting in touch (perhaps you think you could help the person in a specific way with a product, service or by putting them in touch with people in your network).

The connection request message should be the starting point – not the end point – for your rapport-building activities.

Once you've had a few rapport-filled interactions with someone online, you're in an ideal position to take your conversation offline with a phone call.

2. Connection request follow-up

Once you've connected with a new contact, prospect or networking connection, it's time to follow-up.

Most people don't do this but it's a great opportunity to reinforce the fact that you're the go-to person in your field and an all-round useful contact to know.

Send them a message thanking them for connecting with you. And reinforcing some or all of the 3 key points mentioned above, as appropriate:

- Offer to help them with relevant information and contacts

- Briefly explain the beliefs and ideas that make you the go-to expert in your field

- Explain your products and services in more detail to them

Remember, do NOT sell to them, unless you have very special reasons for doing so.

The key should be on thanking them, showing an interest in who they are and what they do (checking their profile is great for this) and helping them with some useful information that reinforces your expert status.

THE POWER OF WEAK TIES

So-called 'weak ties' are business contacts you know 'a bit'. And science shows that the more of them you have, the better.

In the words of Stanford University professor Mark Granovetter:

"Individuals with few weak ties will be deprived of information from distant parts of the social system and will be confined to the provincial news and views of their close friends.

"This deprivation will not only insulate them from the latest ideas and fashions but may put them at a disadvantaged position in the labour market where advancement can depend on knowing about openings at just the right time."

3. Messages to potential contacts in groups

When you join a group on Linkedin, you then gain the on-going opportunity to send people in the group a message.

This is a great option. The message means you have virtually unlimited text to explain who you are, why you're getting in touch and how you think you might be able to help the person in the future.

With a standard connection request, you're limited to 300 characters – not a lot of time to make a great impression with a new potential contact.

I'd recommend including the following points in your initial message sent through Linkedin groups:

- How you met and/or found their profile

- A reference to who you know that they also now (take a look at their profile to find out)

- Any shared interests or activities (take a look at their profile to find out)

- A reason why you're getting in touch (perhaps you think you could help the person in a specific way with a product, service or by putting them in touch with people in your network)

Don't forget, you can also ask to connect with them too, which is about getting their buy-in to an on-going relationship.

Sending a message containing the phrase "with your permission, would it be OK if I sent an invitation to connect on Linkedin?" is a great way to do this.

If you aren't connected to a prospect you want to talk to, finding them in a group and sending them a message is a great means of communication.

So where is all this being 'known' taking you? As we saw in the previous chapter, there are very good scientific reasons why becoming known by as many people as possible is a good idea.

And having a large Linkedin network opens up all kinds of great opportunities for you.

As the late great salesman and motivational speaker Zig Ziglar explained, one of the best ways to get where you want to go is to help other people get where *they* want to go.

And Linkedin can be a powerful tool in helping you do just that.

You might be sat there reading this and wondering how. Let me explain . . .

You know how they say that it's not what you know, but who you know that counts?

So if you can put other people in touch with people that can help them in business, you can help them in a big way, right?

Absolutely. Passing on referrals and putting people in contact with each other is a great way to help people in your business network.

It helps other people out. And positions you as a helpful and well-connected person who's extremely useful to know.

Linkedin can be a powerful tool in helping you to help other people out more quickly, more easily and more often.

Becoming a super-connector

So-called 'super-connectors' are people who know LOTS of people and make useful and targeted introductions to people they want to help.

There are people who effectively work as super-connectors.

They're usually extremely well-connected people that (either directly or indirectly) put people in touch with people who are useful to them in business and then (directly or indirectly) earn a fee as a result.

The world of investment is full of people who introduce entrepreneurs to potential investors on a paid-for basis.

One of the problems of being a super-connector is remembering all the people you know, understanding exactly what they do and who it would be helpful for them to speak to.

And that's where Linkedin can help.

By using the advanced search function on Linkedin, you can quickly pinpoint people in your network who possess particular skills, experience or other key criteria that will help you make more useful connections.

The advanced search function allows you to search through the hundreds or perhaps thousands of people in your network and find the best people to introduce to a particular contact.

As mentioned previously when talking about looking for new prospects, the advanced search tool lets you search through your contacts according to the following criteria:

- Keywords
- First name
- Last name
- Job title
- Company
- School
- Location

In truth, the keywords, job title and location options are by far the most useful options.

For example, imagine you have a contact who wants to speak to lawyers specialising in human rights within 10 miles of Manchester.

You can search through your network for the keywords 'human rights', the job title 'lawyer' and the location postcode M1 to check if you know any suitable introductions.

You can then make introductions via Linkedin itself. Making introductions via Linkedin – rather than email – is great because it allows people to get a much stronger sense of who the person being introduced is.

For a start, there's a picture of them. There's also a summary giving them a clear description of what that person does and recommendations explaining what other people think of the service they offer.

You can either put people in touch on the basis that you are proactively recommending one or the others services.

Or, alternatively, you can introduce people on the basis that you think it might simply be useful for them to connect on Linkedin – without explicitly endorsing either person's services.

This is a good option because you may not want to directly recommend a particular person as you may not have direct experience of their service.

You may simply want to be helpful to both parties to see if/how you can help out by making targeted introductions that the people involved are free to follow-up as and if necessary.

Top tips for becoming a super-connector

Here are some top tips for becoming a super-connector:

1. Make helping others through targeted introductions a key focus of your networking and community building.

2. When you meet people or welcome new people into your network, ask them how you could help them.

It's the quickest way to uncover their needs and get the information you need to propose a solution.

3. Build your Linkedin network around an idea or theme. That way, more people in your network will benefit from introductions.

For example, if you're an accountant in Worcester, you can make it the mission of your network to connect with and bring together as many pro-active owner-managed business people in your town as possible.

People in your network will therefore be more likely to have a shared interest in achieving entrepreneurial success.

4. Always be connecting. Once a week, ask yourself who you've met recently who might benefit from an introduction to someone in your network.

By continually building your network and making introductions, you rapidly increase the number of people who know, like and trust you.

And seeing as people like to do business with people they know, like and trust, it quickly increases the number of people you have as potential customers too!

So if you do nothing else on Linkedin, keep building the number of people that you're connected to and wherever you can, get in touch with them.

Send them a personal connection request and a follow-up message to welcome them into your network.

In a world where people buy people, taking the time to show interest in your network pays huge dividends.

MORNING MOTIVATION

"The mind is the only limit. As long as the mind can envision the fact, then you can do it." – **Arnold Schwarzenegger**

"That dream belongs to you. So go out there and make it a reality." – **Rich Gaspari**

"You've only got 3 choices in life: Give up, give in or give it all you've got." – **Rowan Atkinson**

"We can't become what we need to by remaining what we are." – **Oprah Winfrey**

"The richest people in the world look for and build networks. Everyone else looks for work." – **Robert Kiyosaki**

"You cannot change your destination over night. But you can change your direction over night." – **Jim Rohn**

"Stop putting pound notes over people's heads. Treat everyone the same. With respect." – **Brad Burton**

"You don't need business experience. All you need is a dream. A vision. A mission. A purpose." – **Michael E. Gerber**

"If you don't know what your passion is, realise that one reason for your existence is to find it." – **Oprah Winfrey**

"Losers are people who are afraid of losing." – **Robert Kiyosaki**

"Business is nothing to do with business. It's to do with people." – **Brad Burton**

What words of wisdom get you motivated for a great day every morning? Let me know . . . @TomMallens #8AMINSPIRATION

WANT AN EASIER LIFE?

Would it make your life easier if your sales team was bringing in more business?

My training courses and conference speeches show your sales team exactly how to do just that.

In three easy steps!

Which means they get the know-how they need to become masters of social selling with Linkedin.

And you get a sales team that's getting more in-bound sales leads, more warm phone calls (rather than awkward cold ones) and more business opportunities.

Just check out the testimonials on page 251 to see what some of my recent customers like you think.

Then drop me a message on tom@tommallens.com or a call on +44(0)1926 678 920 to find out how your team could get more leads too.

CHAPTER 4

Real examples of what you can expect

WHAT WORKS BEST FOR YOU IN SALES?

Do you have hints or tips that help you beat gatekeepers?

Or specific questions about anything in this book?

Drop me a line on Linkedin or Twitter

And I'll do my best to answer!

www.linkedin.com/in/TomMallens
@TomMallens #GetPastTheGatekeeper

So hands up if you're sat there reading this and you're wondering what these supposedly huge dividends mentioned at the end of the last chapter are?

Gone on. Be honest!

As we've already seen, there are some powerful social science reasons why being known by more people outside your immediate network of close connections – or 'strong ties' as professor Mark Granovetter would call them – is a good idea.

There are deep-seated psychological reasons why people are just as willing to help people that know someone they know, as they are their regular colleagues and contacts.

And more importantly, why it's more likely that you'll benefit from these kinds of 'weak ties' or casual acquaintances and loose connections.

In my case – as we saw in Chapter 2 – it was Linkedin that helped me get to know the Irish academic that gave me my big break in manufacturing sales with an offer to speak in front of 32 of Europe's largest automotive and aerospace seating manufacturers.

I didn't have to know him like a best friend, just enough for him to get a sense of who I was and where my expertise lay.

With a well-written profile and lots of evidence that you really do know what you're talking about in your work life, Linkedin is brilliant for this.

Without that loose connection made by spreading awareness of who I am and what I do, the opportunity would never have happened.

Just think about all the opportunities that could come your way if more people knew who you were and understood the benefits that working with you delivered.

Yes, you can go and press the flesh at exhibitions, events and networking groups where you'll meet 10, 20 or 30 people at a time.

Social media turbo-charges awareness of who you are and what you do faster than you could ever do in person.

And if more people know what you do and why it's valuable, there's a higher chance they'll engage you when the time is right for them to buy.

It was building awareness of who I was with specific and relevant individuals in organisations that allowed me to start getting appointments at companies that were rejecting my cold calls when I tried to get in via the front desk.

If you use Linkedin effectively and consistently, it's an incredible tool for developing your or your company's brand and ensuring the right people know who you are.

And don't forget this works synergistically with your other marketing efforts.

One of the biggest misconceptions I see with B2B social media platforms like Linkedin is that they're a separate part of your sales and marketing efforts.

According to this misconception, you go to the office and do your work; then, afterwards, you go and do some social media networking to look for prospects.

In fact, it's when your social networking and your other online and offline marketing work together with a consistent message about the benefits you bring that the real power of Linkedin kicks in.

It's like adding rocket fuel to normal word-of-mouth awareness.

Over the following months and years, Linkedin delivered a great stream of leads, warm sales calls and opportunities for me to promote our range of manufacturing raw materials and machinery.

It triggered discussions with managing directors of manufacturing companies both in the UK and throughout Europe.

Conversations I'm certain would NEVER have happened if I'd just tried calling up their receptions out of the blue.

In many cases they saw or liked conversations in relevant Linkedin groups and then got in touch, giving me their mobile numbers.

In every case, I knew a warm and more productive sales call was on the cards as a result of my Linkedin activity.

I no longer had to worry about spending minutes explaining why I was calling to a suspicious gatekeeper looking to end my call.

Among the range of manufacturing products we sell at Fibrecore are various items for the textiles and garment making industries.

We decided that some of the major High Street clothes retailers – and one VERY well known one in particular – were key targets for us.

If we could find the right contacts in the company, perhaps we could get the chance to present our products to them.

Experience told me that phoning the reception of a major multi-national clothing retailer asking if we could come and do a presentation for their senior buying and technical teams was about as time-efficient and likely to succeed as waiting in line to buy tickets for an already sold out One Direction concert.

What we needed was a contact on the inside.

We didn't have one.

But what we did have – and what you also have – was a business directory that would tell us who we knew that knew someone at said High Street clothing retailer (I'm talking about Linkedin if you haven't guessed already).

I found a connection that knew a technical contact at the company and got in touch.

The contact, Sam, worked at a lighting company in the Midlands.

Frustratingly she was not someone I'd ever met. So asking her to help me out might seem unlikely to work.

However, we did have a good mutual friend in common.

Knowing that weak ties can be extremely powerful contacts, I got in touch.

This is where making an effective approach is so vital on Linkedin – and so many people go wrong.

Simply asking for help from strangers is not likely to succeed.

But mentioning your mutual connections with new contacts is a powerful and fast way to quickly build rapport.

So learning how to word your messages to make them as persuasive as possible is important.

Before we knew it we had a red-hot referral to Sam's contact Deborah on the inside at the clothing retailer.

It turned out Deborah was good friends with Sam and she was happy to help organize an opportunity for us.

The next thing we knew, we were displaying our textile products in the heart of the company's London HQ as part of a 4-week display.

The great thing about this process of finding people who can put you in touch with the influencers and businesses you want to speak to is that it's INCREDIBLY time-efficient.

You can literally sit down for half and hour and rattle through a dozen requests to speak to key people with the power to open doors for you and your business.

The irresistible offer

An extension of this tactic is what I call the irresistible offer strategy.

A good contact and great guy called Nick – one of the Midlands' leading leadership trainers – is a huge fan of it.

Rather than focus on nurturing a community of contacts, Nick uses Linkedin to search for new prospects in a super-time-efficient manner; one that really emphasis the benefits of B2B social media for being better known by the people that matter to you in business.

Normally, if you're not connected to someone on Linkedin, you can't send them a message.

If they don't accept your connection request, you have no opportunity to become known by them.

However, as mentioned, if you're in the same group, you CAN send them a message – even though you're not connected and they're not part of your network.

This means you can join a group full of prospective customers and send them messages with a so-called 'irresistible offer'.

You can sit down with a glass of wine in front of the TV and metaphorically knock on the door of the people who could give you business by sending them a message with an offer that's too good for them to ignore.

If they do ignore it, you know they're not interested and there's no point wasting your time pursuing them as a prospect.

If they respond in any way, you know you have a warm sales call lined up.

You know they're interested and you can more easily arrange a meeting or move them along the sales funnel.

The key to making this work is that the initial offer has to be really compelling.

You should not be selling to these people that you message in groups.

Instead, you're contacting them with a fantastic opportunity that allows them to profit and you to start a sales conversation.

In Nick's case, he offers a free place on one of his leadership courses.

If the person likes it – and having been on one I'm sure they will – the company will want to send more people and then, they pay the usual price.

For Nick, those minutes spent messaging prospects start sales conversations worth thousands of pounds.

The important point is he is becoming known by the right people and he is getting in touch with an irresistible offer – not a sales pitch!

One of the great things about using B2B social media to super-charge the number of relevant people who know you is that it throws up all kinds of new opportunities that you otherwise wouldn't know about.

I noticed a B2B sales manager from a well-known satellite TV service on Linkedin and thought he might benefit from some tips on how Linkedin could help his sales team.

Rather than call cold, I got a warm introduction from a mutual contact using Linkedin.

As almost always happens following an introduction from a mutual contact, a highly productive and enjoyable phone conversation followed.

During our chat, Jon mentioned that he was heavily involved in mixed martial arts (MMA) fighting – and had been since he was a youngster.

When I decided about three months later to take part in my first boxing match, I knew Jon was the man I wanted to help me with my training.

Three months later, Jon had pushed me beyond any levels of fitness I'd previously thought I could achieve, taken a broken nose in sparring with the good nature of a consummate gentleman, and prepared me psychologically to the point I felt I could walk through a brick wall.

Thanks to Jon, I won the fight.

It was the first time I'd thrown punches in my life.

The more people you know, the more opportunities you have to build rapport with the people that can help you tackle your next challenge in life, whether it's business or personal.

Remember the process; be known, be liked, be trusted.

It's that simple. The more people you can get to know, the more people among that group will like you and your products, and the more people you can build trust with to facilitate better and more productive business relationships.

As you'll see in the coming chapters, social media can play a massive part in becoming better liked and trusted by your prospects.

But if they don't know you in the first place, you can't start that process.

So get out there and start building your Linkedin network.

Unless you have special reasons to do with confidentiality, the bigger your network is the better.

Identify the types of ideal customer, referral partner and influencer you want in your network and then build your network with as many of them as possible.

They say that if performers, comedians, speakers and other kinds of service-provider can find 2,000 people who love what they do and want to buy every product or service they sell, they can set themselves up for life from that foundation.

Even if your product costs just £1 and you sold one product a month to every customer, you'd have a sustainable income.

Most people sell products worth a lot more than £1.

And while you probably work in B2B sales – not comedy or music – it illustrates the power of an engaged pool of customers who know, like and trust you and recognise you as the go-to expert in your field.

So whatever you do, always be building your network of contacts on social media.

> It's these networks that will sustain you and your business when you want to go fishing for leads or selling new products to existing customers.

Some people say that your most valuable asset in business is your database.

But it's people that make up that database. And they can't be on it if they don't know you.

So don't miss out on an ocean of potential leads by ignoring an online business directory with – at the time of publishing – more than 300,132,846 members around the world.

Get on Linkedin and start becoming known by your existing and potential customers!

People ONLY do business with people they:

1. Know

2. Like

3. Trust

So get out there and start socialising!

MORNING MOTIVATION

"The only thing standing between you and your goal is the bullshit story you keep telling yourself as to why you can't achieve it."
– **Jordan Belfort**

"To move the world, we must first move ourselves." – **Socrates**

"My focus is to forget the pain of life. Forget the pain, mock the pain, reduce it. And laugh." – **Jim Carey**

"If you judge a fish by its ability to climb a tree, it will live its whole life believing it is stupid." – **Albert Einstein**

"Instead of wondering when your next vacation is, set up a life you don't need to escape from." – **Seth Godin**

"Notice that the stiffest tree is easily cracked while the bamboo survives by bending with the wind." – **Bruce Lee**

"Defeat is not the worst of failures. Not to have tried is the true failure." – **George Edward Woodberry**

"Be. Don't try to become." - **OSHO**

"Un-being dead isn't being alive." - **E.E. Cummings**

"No man is a failure who is enjoying life." – **William Feather**

"Our entire life consists ultimately in accepting ourselves as we are."
– **Jean Anouilh**

"The true measure of a person is how he treats a person who can do him absolutely no good." - **Ann Landers**

What words of wisdom get you motivated for a great day every morning? Let me know . . . @TomMallens #8AMINSPIRATION

WANT AN EASIER LIFE?

Would it make your life easier if your sales team was bringing in more business?

My training courses and conference speeches show your sales team exactly how to do just that.

In three easy steps!

Which means they get the know-how they need to become masters of social selling with Linkedin.

And you get a sales team that's getting more in-bound sales leads, more warm phone calls (rather than awkward cold ones) and more business opportunities.

Just check out the testimonials on page 251 to see what some of my recent customers like you think.

Then drop me a message on tom@tommallens.com or a call on +44(0)1926 678 920 to find out how your team could get more leads too.

CHAPTER 5

The incredible power
of being you

We've seen so far that the foundation of making social media an effective tool in your B2B sales efforts is to get out there and be known.

It's no different from real life. Except Linkedin will help you accumulate, engage and manage far more relationships than you could possibly do in the same amount of time face-to-face.

It's like pouring petrol on a fire. You still need the fire to get started. But Linkedin is a powerful fuel to turn your business relationships into a towering inferno.

The more of the right people you know in business on social media, the more opportunities you'll have to meet the people that can help you get where you want to go.

And the more people you can in turn help where they want to go.

It's a virtuous circle. Get it turning, keep it spinning and you're on a high-speed social unicycle to success.

So now that more and more people know who you are and the benefits you offer in business, it's time for the second step in that three-part process of being known, being liked and being trusted.

If people know you, it's no guarantee that they'll want to do business with you.

Why? Because they simply might not like you.

They won't tell you this of course but deep down it's the reason so many potential business opportunities never get off the ground.

I used to – mistakenly – believe that this only applied to businesses that sold services, where the human touch was paramount in quantifying the benefits of the largely intangible item being sold.

I especially believed this when I started working in the manufacturing sector, selling large items of machinery and capital equipment.

The machinery either did or didn't do what the company wanted, I thought.

I could not have been more wrong.

Perhaps you've been there yourself? They won't return your calls. They don't respond to emails.

If people don't like you, they will find a reason to shop elsewhere.

You get the feeling that you're an unwanted nuisance to them – which does nothing to help your confidence and sales success.

There are very few truly unique products where no possible alternative product or service that performs a similar function exists.

If the person you need to speak to doesn't like you, they will simply find an alternative option.

And they'll convince themselves that the alternative option is actually better than the option you offer.

You can shout 'til you're blue in the face that your revolutionary new pocket-sized inflatable tractor is a better product than the competition's pocket-sized inflatable tractor.

But your words will fall on deaf ears.

I was speaking to the former head of change at a credit card company who explained how he was in charge of an IT project.

He had to oversee selection and installation of a new IT system; a contract worth more than a million pounds.

After narrowing a list of possible companies down to four or five, he had to make the final decision based on which company would do the best job.

How did he make the decision in the face of endless data about how the different companies' IT solutions would perform?

As he explained to me, ultimately he went with the company whose salesman overseeing the project he liked the most.

Sure, he justified the decision to his colleagues based on facts and figures.

But the real reason was based on who he liked the most. It was an entirely emotional decision justified with facts after the decision had already been made.

I'm suggesting that ultimately most decisions are made in this way – based on emotions and justified with facts afterwards.

Emotion is crucial in any sales situation. Without it, the sale will not be completed.

Usually, it's a positive emotion; the customer is excited or reassured at the prospect of buying from you.

And occasionally it's a negative emotion that you convert into a positive one through good negotiation, objection-handling and customer care.

If after a number of discussions, there is still zero emotion between you, the potential customer and the product, you cannot sell to that person. It means they are indifferent and completely disinterested.

If, on the other hand, that person has strong positive emotions about your product you can use them to your advantage.

And it's sometimes possible that strong negative emotions can be addressed and used to build a case to answer their concerns and prove them wrong.

A total absence of emotion is the kiss of death for the sale.

If you're going to do business with Mrs Singh, the head of purchasing at Globo-Corporation, it's vital that on some level, she likes something about you.

If you're going to make social media work for you, it's vital that on some level, your ideal potential customers like something about you too.

And the best and easiest way to be liked on social media?

Be yourself! Or, more accurately, be the best, strongest and most excellent version of yourself.

Be the person you are when you're at your best in a sales situation.

The reason is simple but important.

If people don't like your updates and character on Linkedin, then the chances are, they're probably not going to like you.

This is great because they're at total liberty to dis-connect with you and sever the social media relationship at any time.

You no longer have to waste time building a relationship with someone who doesn't like you and, therefore, is highly unlikely to ever want to do business with you anyway.

I remember a local Midlands-based entrepreneur called Nigel being asked if he worried about sending out so much email marketing (Nigel sends out a LOT of emails).

Not at all, he explained. If people don't like it, they're almost certainly not the kind of pro-active, get-up-and-go people that are most likely to buy his products and services.

So why waste time on them. They're never going to buy anyway, without MASSIVE effort to convert them.

There are plenty more prospects out there that will be much easier to convert because they don't just like Nigel, they LOVE him.

I met a great guy called Peter who ran the regional operations of a local business networking franchise.

Peter shared a powerful anecdote that perfectly sums this up.

Peter was a former high-level corporate finance specialist – with a penchant for technicolor shirts that made my eyes want to bleed – at a huge multi-national packaging company.

He recalled how his boss had told him during a meeting after he landed a huge new contract: "You were lucky there. We've been trying to sell our product to that company for years."

Peter explained that the reason his boss hadn't been able to "sell that product" to the company was precisely because of this attitude.

Peter's boss wanted to dump his product onto the customer at all costs.

Peter on the other hand wanted to help the customer by building the strongest, most mutually-beneficial and most like-able relationship with the customer that he could.

In the end, the customer didn't want to go anywhere else to buy. Peter and his company's product was the only man for them because they liked him more than anyone else.

In the end, the numbers and data on whose product is best will tell you whatever the people involved want it to.

With this necessity of being likeable on social media in mind, it's important to avoid one cardinal sin: Being bland, boring and invisible.

If you're loud, boisterous and direct, be loud, boisterous and direct on social media.

If you're all flowers, fairies and positive energy, be all flowers, fairies and positive energy on social media.

If you're like a piece of bland white bread, there's nothing for people to like or loathe about you.

You'll drown into the depths of Linkedin updates among an ocean of generic business articles, never to be seen again.

But stand out through the power of your own unique personality and some people will like you and some people won't.

I signed up for email newsletters from a US entrepreneur called Dan.

His claim to fame was that he started his first company with $840 and turned it into more than $450 million during the 1980s.

He now has a net worth valued at more than $50 billion.

More importantly he's the only person I've met whose email newsletters feature phrases such as "why the fuck aren't you going after your dream" and "I hope you're ripping the ass out of 2014".

Some people will find this language offensive.

Some people will absolutely love it.

Dan builds his current business as a mentor for super-ambitious entrepreneurs around the people that love it.

He doesn't worry about the people that find it offensive.

In the same way, if you're true to yourself and some people like you while others feel you're not for them, it's great news.

You can now worry about the people that like you and nurture your relationships with them.

You can like their comments, share their content and register on their radar every time you log on to Linkedin.

You don't have to be controversial and polarise opinion.

But you do have to give people something to either like or dislike.

Otherwise, you'll be forgotten in an instant.

Have you ever heard those statistics that most people don't buy on the 1st or 2nd approach from a salesperson?

But DO buy on the 6th, 7th or 8th contact? Interactions on social media absolutely count towards that total of approaches and engagement.

And the more authentic and true to yourself they are the better.

If you're not sure what to say on social media, ask yourself what you'd say if a group of your customers were in the room.

And then say that.

If you've become known by the right people and built a network full of contacts it's useful for you to speak to, then this is exactly what you'll be doing whenever you update your Linkedin status.

Taking the heart of what makes you liked by a particular type of person or potential customer and harnessing it in a focused and methodical way to appeal to more of those same types of people is the essence of personal branding.

You may have heard the term used by image consultants who stress that having a consistent and distinctive look is an important tool for getting ahead in business.

The best image consultants don't just focus on how you look, they focus on every aspect of how you act to create a coherent story that people can buy into – in the same way that people buy into consumer brands.

Personal branding is about marketing yourself as if you were a product.

It's about packaging your career history, look, behavior, ideas, experience and actions into a unified concept that – like a branded product on a supermarket shelf – people can choose to buy or not.

In the case of a personal brand, they'll either buy into your story and take a liking to you and your products or they won't.

People not liking your personal brand is totally fine because there are millions of people out there and whatever industry you're in, there will be ideal potential customers that DO like your personal brand.

Here are three important personal branding mistakes you'll want to avoid if you want to stand out and be liked by the right people in business for the right reasons:

Mistake 1. Be fake

If you're the life and soul of the party on Linkedin and the dullest thing since tinned mackerel face-to-face, people will sense something is wrong.

Likewise, if you're a larger-than-life, gag-a-minute funny-machine in reality and a bland carbon copy of a grey and miserable salesperson online, you won't create the consistent brand that's needed to get results. People will sense the inauthenticity and they won't like it.

Remember Milli Vanilli and Lance Armstrong? Being fake cost them everything. Try not to do it.

Like Great White sharks and blood, people can smell inconsistency a mile away. And subconsciously, they'll pounce on it as a reason not to trust you.

Which, as you can imagine, does not do your sales prospects much good.

Mistake 2. Be half-hearted

Great brands are not half-hearted. McDonald's and Coca Cola are in your face whether you like it or not.

Whatever you think of them, they stand for something and they make it known.

If you want to stand out for something in your industry by creating a strong personal brand, then you might as well go all in.

This means some people might not like what you stand for or they simply might not like you.

This is fine. All the great brands create a negative reaction in some people.

You cannot truly connect with and attract some people if you're not willing to disconnect with and deter some people too.

If you try to please everyone, you end up pleasing no-one.

I spoke to the director of a national chain of networking groups called Brad.

Brad has an extremely strong personal brand. It's built on his irrepressible energy, straight-talking and in-your-face style.

Brad works at a million miles an hour and says what he thinks in a very straight-to-the-point way.

He fills Facebook with pictures of his business success and of him going out and getting shit-faced (his words!) with other business people.

Some people don't like his (extremely) strong opinions on everything from women serving in the army to what other business people are doing wrong.

And other people love them. Brad doesn't worry about people that don't like his ideas and opinions. He focuses his time, energy and effort on those that do.

And his business success speaks for itself.

Mistake 3. Be inconsistent

If you're going to stand out as the go-to person in your industry for a particular type of product, system, idea or service, you won't get results if you're chopping and changing every 5 minutes.

This means being consistent in your branding, promotional and networking activities.

A business coach named Andy once told me the ultimate formula for success (S).

It was, he said, simply a case of taking massive action (MA), of the right type, or 'right stuff' as he called it (RS), consistently (C) over time.

So, for fans of algebra out there, you can sum up the formula for success in life as:

$$MA + RS \times C = S$$

That C is important. Word-of-mouth referrals, introductions and opportunities will not spring up as the result of one or two bits of activity.

They will start to come flooding in only as a result of consistent activity over time.

Mistake 4. Be only online

I stress this point a lot in the social sales workshops I run. Linkedin, or social media networking in general, is not a new activity to add to the list of things you should be doing.

Platforms like Linkedin, Twitter and Facebook, are simply tools to help you achieve greater results from the networking, branding, marketing and selling work that you should be doing already!

It's a subtle but crucial difference.

It just so happens that for B2B salespeople in manufacturing, technology and IT industries, Linkedin is by far the best platform for getting more leads, beating gate-keepers and finding new business opportunities.

But it's going to work much more effectively if you're already out there looking for more leads, trying to beat gate-keepers and find new business opportunities anyway.

I met a salesman who complained that he didn't have as many customers as he'd like and wanted to use Linkedin to get more.

The problem was, he simply wasn't doing enough activity offline, let alone online with social media.

Use it effectively and Linkedin will get results.

But like all marketing, it works much more effectively in synergy with other marketing channels too; whether that's direct mail, trade exhibitions, email campaigns, PR, trade press or beyond.

Whatever you do, don't think of personal branding as something you do only online.

For it to work, you have to do it consistently online and in person too.

In the next chapter, we'll look at how you can be liked on social media in practice and what the key steps to making Linkedin work for you really are!

WIN A CHANCE OF A MYSTERY PRIZE!

If you take a pic of yourself with your copy of
Get Past The Gatekeeper and mention me on Linkedin or Twitter,
then each month, you'll be entered into a prize draw to win a
cool mystery prize.

So get snapping those selfies now!

www.linkedin.com/in/TomMallens
@TomMallens #GetPastTheGatekeeper

CHAPTER 6

How to create your perfect Linkedin profile

ARE YOU IN SALES?

Do you get frustrated when your calls aren't put through to key decision-makers?

Or do you wish more clients would come to you – instead of you chasing them?

If so, you can get 37 tried and tested ways to win more business-to-business sales leads in my exclusive free report.

Tips 5, 12 and 29 will help most salespeople ditch awkward cold calls AND get more in-bound leads more quickly and easily than ever.

They're the same tips that landed sales and marketing manager Hana Smiddy £60,000 of new business opportunities within days.

So don't miss out, download your copy now at:

www.tommallens.com/moreleadsfromlinkedin

We've seen so far that the foundation to great social selling is leveraging your personal brand and using this in combination with your other 'normal' sales techniques and strategies.

In other words, you use social media to become known by more of the right people with a likeable personal brand that will encourage them to know, like and trust you.

But how do you create a likeable profile on Linkedin?

This is one of the most popular parts of my training courses because people love to create their little piece of social media real estate and get it right.

However, the important thing to realise from a social sales perspective is that your Linkedin profile shouldn't really be about you at all.

If you want to get the best results, it should be about your customers!

Of course, the information is about you, but the focus and the language you use should be written entirely with your ideal potential customer in mind.

To create a perfect Linkedin profile that helps you attract in-bound leads, warm phone calls and more business opportunities you need to answer one question.

Why on earth would anyone in their right mind want to give you their money?

This is extremely important because most people get so caught up in writing their profiles that they forget one important truth in life: No-one is interested in you.

OK, that might be a little harsh, but when it comes to sales and business, generally speaking, most people are most interested in themselves.

Which means that if they read your Linkedin profile, they don't want to be reading about how wonderful you are.

They want to read how you can help them, solve their problems and make their lives easier.

Like so much in business, it's not about you, it's about the customer!

So if you can answer this clearly, concisely and memorably you're on the road to a powerful social media presence.

The 5 steps to Linkedin profile perfection

There are 5 key parts to get right for an effective Linkedin profile – and don't forget that these fundamentally apply to most other social media platforms too.

Part 1: Your photograph

A professional photo can be used on all your personal branding/marketing material and gives consistency across different social media and online platforms. It helps create a consistent image of brand YOU.

Having a decent photograph that reflects your personality and brand helps humanize you and can make you stand out for all the right reasons.

So ask yourself if your photograph accurately reflects the image you want to project to the outside world?

Is it crisp, clean and professional? Are you even looking at the camera?

Or does it look like it was taken on a mobile phone at 3am outside a nightclub?

Was it actually taken at 3am outside a nightclub?

Are you holding a gun? Are you standing with a llama in a library? Do you look like your picture should be in a phone booth in Soho?

The reason I ask is because I've seen plenty of examples where people are outside nightclubs at 3am, holding guns and one where someone really was standing with a llama in a library.

If any of those things are strong parts of your personal brand then your photo is perfect.

If it's NOT (which it almost certainly isn't) then it's best to ditch the photo of the llama or gun and invest in a decent professional picture.

A couple of years ago I was searching for contacts in the automotive sector when I found a senior purchasing director at a major luxury car manufacturer whose Linkedin profile photograph was him dressed as a wizard. And not just a 'bit' of a wizard.

I'm talking full-on Merlin-meets-Gandalf-meets-Dumbledore complete with an owl, a castle in the background and a mini solar system spinning magically in the palm of his hand.

If you're a BIG, BOLD and BRASH character, why blend in with a boring photograph that makes you look like an accountant.

On the other hand, if you're reliable, dependable and super-organised, make sure your photograph conveys this image too.

Sarah was a sales manager for a company that makes safety inspection cameras for the oil and gas industry.

I met her after we connected on Linkedin to help the company with its social sales strategy.

Sarah is a colourful character and captured her personality with a memorable photo.

It was of her grinning from ear-to-ear clutching her pony tails.

It was completely black-and-white except for a bright pink cowboy hat she was wearing.

The fact that I remember it to this day years after our meeting proves that standing-out from the crowd helps you be remembered for the right reasons.

2. Professional headline

This is the job description that shows up next to your photograph and underneath your name at the top of your Linkedin profile.

By default, Linkedin picks up the title from your most recent job for this section. However, you can change it to whatever you want. You get 120 characters of text.

When you fill this section out, remember that the objective is to encourage the people that you want to speak to (usually potential customers) to want to speak to you in return.

Don't forget that generally speaking, no-one wants to speak to a B2B salesman, a lawyer, an accountant or an IFA.

If your professional headline says simply your job title, you're not maximizing the perception of the value you offer.

On the other hand, people definitely do want to speak to key influential people in their industry who can solve their problems.

They want the opportunity to build relationships with people who have:

- Access to business opportunities
- Access to other influential people
- Know-how that gives them a business advantage

Instead of saying what you do, think about the value and benefits you bring to the people you work with and use the 120 characters to sum this up in a compelling word-bite.

Getting the right keywords that your customers are searching for online into your professional headline is a great way to make yourself more easily findable by and visible to potential customers too.

Your photograph, name and professional headline are the three bits of information that show up first in Linkedin (and Google searches). So it's worth getting them right.

If you're not sure where to start, use the following structure as a guide:

- What you do
- Who you help and the problems you solve
- Other relevant keywords

Being able to concisely sum up what you do is crucial to successful networking.

One of the big reasons people might fail to pass on referrals is because they don't fully understand what you do.

Getting your Linkedin professional headline right is a great opportunity to do that.

Take a moment to write out your professional headline. Remember, this is a word-bite of brand YOU.

Your professional headline:

3. Summary

Next up is your summary. This is your chance to grab the attention of anyone that reads your profile.

If you get it right, by the time someone finishes reading it, they'll be sold on the idea that speaking to you is a great idea.

Get it wrong, which most people do, and they'll give up reading within the first few words without ever being interested in who you are, what you do, and how you could help them.

There is some terrible advice out there regarding writing Linkedin profiles.

Many people have been told to start writing their profiles by thanking people for looking at their summary section.

Their profiles will start something like this:

Hello. Thank you for looking at my profile.

I help companies install cloud computing systems so they can manage their data more effectively and securely.

This is, frankly, terrible advice. It's usually given by people that don't have any understanding of what makes for good copywriting.

People's attention spans are horribly short and the words 'Hello. Thank you for looking at my profile' do not grab anyone's attention these days.

Then, it's followed by someone talking about themselves which, as mentioned, people are NOT interested in.

Just to stress the point again (because it's extremely important), people are – in marketing terms at least – only interested in one person; themselves.

You must write your Linkedin profile about your ideal customer. Not about you.

That's why, for a perfectly structured profile that will help you grab the interest of customers, I highly recommend using the following so-called 6P structure.

This is a structure based around 6 words all beginning with P that help you create a fantastic Linkedin profile summary section that appeals to your ideal target customer.

But before you do, it's worth pointing out that these 6 Ps are the foundation of amazing marketing copy in general.

If you start to look around at marketing copy in brochures, magazines, leaflets, or even the scripts for TV adverts, you'll notice that the best ones follow this kind of structure, either exactly or in an adapted form.

In either case, the best examples of marketing copy take the key elements of the following structure and combine them in a way that's right for the task in hand.

So take note and keep an eye out for this structure in adverts, promotions and broadcasts you see, hear or read.

Position – What is the current position, or status quo, of your ideal customer? This is your chance to show them that you understand their world.

It's often said that the key to successful marketing is knowing your customer better than they know themselves.

In that case, the position section of your profile is your chance to show just a little of quite how amazingly well you know your ideal customer.

Be as specific as possible. If you want to stand out from the crowd on Linkedin (and in business in general), being a specialist is important.

Saying you're an accountant is not very memorable. Few people will understand the types of people you want to speak to.

Saying that you're an accountant who specializes in helping R&D-focused manufacturing businesses between £1 million and £5 million turnover within 50 miles of Manchester makes it easier for people to understand exactly what you do and makes it easier for them to recommend the right kind of prospects to you when they meet them.

The position section of your profile is your chance to show your ideal prospects that you understand their world by telling them what their position is. It's about reminding people of the status quo, as it exists now.

For example, you might say: *As the director of a multi-million pound automotive logistics company, you'll know that IT systems are crucial to fulfilling orders on time.*

Or: *As operations director for a carbon fibre composites company, you'll know that your ability to process material quickly is crucial to increasing output and getting a return on your machinery assets.*

If you get this section right, when someone matching your ideal customer profile reads it, they will see immediately that you understand their world.

They'll understand that, of all the people out there offering similar types of product or service, you're the only one that truly understands them and their world; the pressures they're under, the difficulties they face and the challenges they want to overcome.

Which puts you right at the front of the queue in their minds when they start thinking about people who could help them.

This first section is about building rapport with your prospect and standing out from the crowd by showing that you have a unique understanding of a particular type of person – one that matches your ideal customer profile.

Problem – As the name suggests, this next section of your profile is about reminding your ideal prospect of the problems they have?

This is where a lot of people will tell you to start writing about your products and services and the problems that they solve.

This is completely wrong.

Writing about the problems your products and services solve and writing about the problems that your prospects face may appear similar at first but it is fundamentally different. Here's why...

People do not buy things purely to experience a benefit.

They buy things to experience a benefit that simultaneously takes away a pain they are experiencing now.

If they do not have pain, they do not need a benefit.

If you're not depressed by cold weather, jealous of your more successful neighbors or frustrated by your cramped living conditions, you don't need a huge and luxurious mansion in the sun.

If you're not depressed, jealous or frustrated with your current conditions, you have no need for the luxury mansion solution that's on offer.

In the same way, for your Linkedin profile summary to be effective in hooking the interest of your ideal customer, you need to remind them of the problems they face BEFORE you explain your solution.

It's only once you've reminded people of how bad the problems they have are, that you can introduce a solution with any hope of them actually wanting to buy it.

If there's no problem, then there's no need for a solution.

So, after showing your ideal customer that you understand them in the first part of your profile, remind them of the problem they face in the second section.

This might be just one or two sentences, for example (following on from the examples in the 'position' section previously:

As the director of a multi-million pound automotive logistics company, you'll know that IT systems are crucial to fulfilling orders on time.

The problem is, most IT systems are not designed around the needs of fast-moving logistics businesses like yours, which means they can't cater for the demands of companies that need data in real-time.

Or, using the example of a profile designed to appeal to the operations directors of carbon fibre composites companies:

As operations director for a carbon fibre composites company, you'll know that your ability to process material quickly is crucial to increasing output and getting a return on your machinery assets.

The trouble is, most systems are extremely slow and focus on needlessly long processing times as a misguided indication of quality. Which means your processing speeds are needlessly long with no improvement in quality as a result.

In both cases, we've shown ideal potential customers that we understand the world they live in and we've reminded them of a problem they face and its impact on them.

The next step, is to talk about the future...

Projection – The projection section of your profile is where you talk about what will happen if the problem goes un-solved.

In other words, you explain to people what the problem will mean for them and what impact it will have.

Not having enough hours in the day to get stuff done is a problem.

But it's not a problem that, on its own, would cause anyone to buy something to solve it.

Reminding people that if they don't do something to eliminate this problem they will become stressed and start to perform poorly at work which will reduce their chance of promotion IS a reason someone might invest time and money in a time-management or productivity tool to eliminate the problem of not having enough hours in the day.

Likewise, another example of projecting the results of a problem if it goes un-solved is to tell them that because they are badly organized and don't have enough hours in the day they will miss out on time with their children which will lead to their children resenting them.

Think about the effects of the problem your ideal customer faces. What will those effects be in the short, medium and long term?

Then remind your prospects of this.

You can be as gentle or as harsh as you like here. You can remind people that they'll lose time and money as a result of not tackling the problem or you can remind people that eventually they'll lose their jobs and end up begging for change on a street corner while their friends stand around laughing at them for becoming a worthless joke.

Gentle or harsh, whichever extreme you feel is right for you is the one you should go with.

Some people are not comfortable with layering on the picture of personal pain to prospects who are learning about your products and services. Some people are.

The key is to simply be consistent with what you say to people face-to-face and in your other marketing material.

Let's use the examples of profiles aimed at directors of automotive logistics companies and operations directors of carbon fibre composites companies again.

Position: *As the director of a multi-million pound automotive logistics company, you'll know that IT systems are crucial to fulfilling orders on time.*

Problem: *The problem is, most IT systems are not designed around the needs of fast-moving logistics business, which means they can't cater for the demands of companies that need data in real-time.*

Projection: *If you continue to rely on systems designed for the needs of other, slower moving industries, you will lose up to 7 seconds on every order which translates to weeks of lost time and up to £17,897 of lost profit every year.*

Or, using the example of a profile designed to appeal to the operations directors of carbon fibre composites companies:

Position: *As operations director for a carbon fibre composites company, you'll know that your ability to process material quickly is crucial to increasing output and getting a return on your machinery assets.*

Problem: *The trouble is, most systems are extremely slow and focus on needlessly long processing times as a misguided indication of quality. Which means your processing speeds are needlessly long with no improvement in quality as a result.*

Projection: *As the popularity of rapid-form thermoplastic composite components continues, if you're stuck using slow processing techniques you will lose a growing number of supply contracts to companies that have invested in faster production methods. Which means you'll have to fight harder and harder for a smaller and smaller share of the composites manufacturing business. Without faster processing equipment, you are on an inevitable path to failure.*

As with all the sections in this 6P structure, the projection section doesn't need to be long.

Just one or two sentences will be enough.

A couple of good sentences that grab the interest of your ideal potential customers and start the process of converting them into customers is better than hundreds of sentences that talk about you and how you're a 'dynamic game-changer' within your industry.

As mentioned, the harsh reality when it comes to social media profiles is that no-one cares about you. They only care about themselves and what you can do to help them.

Which is where (finally) your product or service comes in . . .

Proposal – Your proposal is not just a description of your product or service.

More importantly, it's your proposal to eliminate the problem you have just outlined to the prospect reading your Linkedin profile.

It's your chance to talk about what you can do to help your prospect overcome the problems they're facing and, very importantly, how they can overcome them too.

A lot of people will jump straight to explaining what their product or service is when they try to write a Linkedin profile summary.

But without a clear picture of the problem it's solving, that information is not helpful to prospects.

It's only in the context of a problem that information about your solution is helpful.

One of the reasons people don't buy is that they're unsure about what they're going to get.

This uncertainty creates fear and fear stops sales dead.

People become afraid that if they buy, they might not get the outcome they're looking for.

They worry that if they buy, it will turn out to be the wrong decision.

This type of worry is the cause of so-called 'buyer's remorse'. It's what happens when people go ahead and buy and then immediately worry they've made the wrong decision.

In many cases, they change their mind and come to you asking for a refund, exchange or some other way of backing out of the sale.

If this has ever happened to you, it's EXTREMELY frustrating.

You think you've done the hard work and can relax and look forward to getting your money, bonus or commission only to have it whisked away from underneath your nose.

Eliminating uncertainty BEFORE the sale goes ahead is one of the key ways to prevent buyer's remorse.

That's one of the (many) reasons McDonald's is so popular. Whatever people think of the food, they know exactly what they're going to get when they buy it – it's exactly the same. EVERY. SINGLE. TIME.

If you buy food at McDonald's you can be certain about what you're going to get.

Taking a sentence or two to explain what your solution looks like and what your customers are going to get is extremely valuable.

Don't just explain what your solution is. Once again, think of it from your customer's point of view.

What does it mean for them? What does it mean from their point of view?

How long does your solution take to deliver? How is it delivered? Is it a one-off solution or an on-going process?

Give people a fuller sense of what the product or service you offer is and what it means for them.

Will they have to do anything in order to get the benefits? Or will the benefits happen automatically without any involvement from them?

Whatever it is, be clear about it. That way, you'll set people's expectations and they'll feel reassured and less uncertain about what they'll get if they buy.

As mentioned, when people feel certain about what they'll get, they feel less afraid of a negative outcome after they buy.

And this in turn makes them much more likely to go ahead and buy – secure in the knowledge that they know exactly what they're going to get.

Which brings us onto the next point. How can you convince potential customers that you really are as good as you say you are?

Proof – It's easy to say you'll deliver great results. In fact, everyone does. I've never met a salesperson yet that said their products didn't do a good job.

The best salespeople don't try to sell when what they have to offer isn't right for a particular type of customer, company or situation.

But they still maintain that what they do will deliver results.

The trouble is, most potential customers out there simply won't believe you.

They know you'll say you're good. Every salesperson they've ever met has said the same thing.

So how can you prove it? How can you convince them that what you offer really does deliver results?

You have to include some proof in your profile. This could be facts and figures that back up your claims.

Or it could be testimonials from customers.

One of the reasons Linkedin is great is because it makes it quick and easy to gather lots of compelling testimonials from customers – to prove that your proposed solution really is as good as you say it is.

And unlike so many testimonials you see, each one has the full name of the person that gave it and a photograph.

This has a powerful psychological effect in making the testimonial seem more believable.

Have you ever seen promotions that featured a testimonial that looked amazing but lacked credibility because it was given by 'Mrs Brown from Bournemouth' or 'John from Manchester'.

Even worse, perhaps you've seen those dodgy promotions that use testimonials from people that are completely anonymous.

"It was amazing and you should definitely buy it," is not very believable when there's no name attached.

Sadly, there are lots of examples of this kind of useless testimonial out there.

Frankly, I suspect the people behind the marketing material in question have just made them up.

Linkedin testimonials are quick and easy to collect and can't be faked – unless you go about creating fake profiles which, to be honest, people in business have better things to do with their time.

There are some big mistakes most people make when gathering testimonials, some quick and easy solutions, which we'll look at in the coming pages.

A Midlands-based marketing guru called Nigel was a big fan of the power of testimonials.

So much so that when he decided to create a promotional brochure for a home-based business franchise he didn't fill it with any conventional marketing information or details about the franchise opportunity.

Instead, he collected hundreds of testimonials from his existing franchise customers talking about how brilliant the business opportunity was.

He then simply gave this booklet packed with hundreds of testimonials to potential customers and only then, after they'd seen it and been amazed by the things existing customers said, did he follow up with specific details about the business opportunity itself.

Testimonials are super-powerful and if you're not regularly asking for them on Linkedin, you could be missing out on some massively powerful marketing collateral.

Please – This is the final part of your perfect Linkedin profile summary.

The please section is your request to the person reading your profile to do something.

In other words, it's your call to action – the thing that every piece of marketing copy should end with.

Remember, this 'section' only needs to be one or two sentences long.

All marketing should end with a call to action because without asking for people to do something, it's 100% certain that they won't do it.

People are busy. They're not going to go to your website or look through your brochure for fun of their own accord.

You have to ask them to do it and give them a reason or benefit.

What you ask people to do in your call to action is up to you.

Perhaps you want them to call you, visit your website or send you an email.

Whatever it is, if you don't ask, they definitely won't do it. So make sure you ask!

Putting it all together

Now that you understand the logic behind the 6 Ps structure, you can start to put it all together to create a compelling Linkedin profile structure that grabs the attention of your ideal potential customers.

Remember, you have up to 2,000 characters so use them. You don't have to use all of them but leaving this section blank not only creates a bad impression (the kind of impression that you can't be bothered to fill it in).

It's also a huge wasted opportunity to get a powerful message to your potential customers.

Just think about it, of the 360 million (and rising rapidly) business people around the world on Linkedin, someone has decided to take a few moments out of their precious day to look at information about YOU.

If you don't have a Linkedin profile summary or it's just badly written and focused on you, you're missing out on a valuable opportunity to influence people in the direction of becoming a customer.

Or, of making them think about the potential customers that they know and could mention to you.

The goal is to come up with a short and sharp message that grabs the reader's attention, makes them appreciate that you understand them, can solve the pressing problems that are causing them unnecessary pain AND have compelling evidence that by working with you, they'll end that pain once and for all.

To give you a flavour, here's a brief example of a Linkedin profile summary featuring all the key elements of the 6Ps structure we've just discussed. In this case, it's for an imaginary software salesman.

If you manage a team of salespeople, you'll know that the more easily your people can get information on customers, the more easily they can sell.

Unfortunately, it's extremely hard to find CRM systems that give sales teams access to important facts and figures quickly and easily while they're out on the road visiting customers.

Which means your team miss opportunities because they're not properly prepared with the facts, figures and information they need when they get through to key-decision makers.

Our CRM interface gives your sales team access to live customer data at the touch of a button from the comfort of your sales reps' cars. It takes three minutes to install and you don't have to do anything. After a 15-minute consultation call, we do all the work and you don't have to lift a finger.

Every single one of our customers who followed our installation process has achieved at least 14% increases in sales within 2 months of installing the system. And you can see the big benefits hundreds of our recent customers have got after installing our software in the testimonials section below.

If you go to XYZ.com, you'll see a 95-second video showing exactly how the software works and you'll get 3 free tips on how you can increase your sales teams' productivity right now too!

Did you spot the 6Ps in there? Hopefully, the position, problem, projection, proposal, proof and please sections were clear.

Of course, you can tailor the structure to your needs or change the tone and style of language, but getting even a little of each of the six Ps into your summary will be a big help.

And simply learning the 6Ps structure will be a big help anytime you want to write persuasive and powerful marketing copy in general.

Other ideas
Other things you can do to add impact to your profile include using special characters – such as ◆◆□◆□□◆□ – to break-up the text and create sub-sections, paragraph breaks and headers.

And don't forget that you can add a touch of your own personality.

In fact, I'd highly encourage it. This is social media after all and one of the ways you get to build up likeability with potential customers is by being yourself, letting your natural sense of humour and personality shine through.

If you're very fun, up-beat and lively, use fun, up-beat and lively language.

If you're serious, mater-of-fact and straight-talking, use serious, mater-of-fact and straight-talking words.

Adding Slideshare and Youtube multi-media to your profile
Linkedin allows you to include a variety of multi-media in your profile.

This is a great way to include extra information for prospects looking at your profile and to make your profile stand out from other people.

You can embed anything from PDFs, PowerPoint presentations, SlideShare documents and YouTube videos in your profile by hitting the upload File button when you're editing your profile.

Slideshare

Slideshare is a file sharing site that allows you to upload content. It is often described as the YouTube of PowerPoint presentations.

It means you can host content (usually PowerPoint presentations and PDFs) online for free.

SlideShare is now owned by Linkedin and because its aim is to share new and useful content, any information you upload is extremely highly rated by Google in terms of SEO.

Uploading content means you have a URL for your company brochure, sales document or other information that you can easily share in emails and other social media sites.

It also makes it easy for people to share your content with their contacts.

YouTube

YouTube is one of the biggest search engines, 2nd only to Google. In fact, it's actually owned by Google. Which makes content on YouTube extremely valuable in terms of SEO.

Videos are a great way to market your business as – if done correctly – they can be extremely memorable and effective.

A personal or company YouTube video explaining your products and services can be a great asset in getting attention from potential customers.

And embedding it into your Linkedin profile is a great way to stand out from the crowd and help people get a sense of whether they might want to do business with you.

4. Recommendations

The fourth step to creating a perfect profile is the recommendations section.

Word of mouth recommendations remain one of the most powerful pieces of marketing collateral you can get.

The good news is that Linkedin makes it quick and easy to request recommendations from everyone you do business with.

Asking people for feedback on your service and getting them to explain what they liked about it by writing a testimonial is a great step to build into your sales cycle.

It's also a valuable touch-point you can use to increase interaction with customers and build your relationships with them.

There are a couple of different ways to ask for recommendations and, once again, most people miss some big opportunities which means they don't get the type or volume or recommendations they'd like.

And they miss out on great marketing material as a result.

Most people simply send a message to their contacts asking if that person can recommend them.

They may or may not get a response. And that response may or may not say something useful about your products or services.

Either way, you're not sure of what you're going to get.

To request a recommendation on Linkedin, you must be connected to that person which, if you've been pro-actively building your network with people you meet in business, you will be.

If not, now's the time to find them and send a connection request – and don't forget to tag them too!

How to get fantastic recommendations
There are two main strategies for getting recommendations on Linkedin, which I'll explain now.

First is a quick and simple way, the second takes a little longer but is, arguably, better in all respects; more effective for you and more helpful for the person giving the recommendation too.

Here's a step-by-step explanation of both:

Strategy 1 – Quick and simple
In both cases, the first step is to simply select the drop down menu on your own profile and follow the on-screen prompts.

Instead of simply sending a message asking people if they can recommend you – which is a bit vague – suggest some specific areas where you'd appreciate their feedback.

If you suggest some areas they might like to mention, you save their thinking time and make it more likely they'll actually write a recommendation in the first place.

Asking people to comment on specific aspects of your products or service means you get much more compelling recommendations that highlight great details of your services, rather than vague statements saying that your service was "really good".

Examples of things you can ask people to comment on include:

- How they found a particular feature or benefit of your product or service

- Whether they'd recommend you to other contacts

- Whether your services matched (or exceeded) their expectations

- If they feel better able to solve the problem they were facing before buying your product

- How they benefitted from working with you

An example might read like the following:

Good to work with you last week. Just wondered if you could share your thoughts on the service and write a recommendation. If you're not sure where to start, perhaps you could you mention:

- *What was the most valuable aspect of the service in terms of cost-savings?*
- *Do you feel better able to manage costs in your business moving forward?*
- *Do you think other managing directors of bio-science firms would benefit from this service? . . .*

Many thanks and best regards, Jag.

After a few days, you should get a notification on Linkedin showing that the person you asked has written a recommendation which you can now publish to your profile at the click of a button.

You get to approve all recommendations before they're made public so you retain control over what's said about you on your profile.

And you can now use that recommendation in your offline marketing too.

Strategy 2 – Most effective
The second option is slightly lengthier but produces better results!

Start by phoning the person you want to recommend you. Let's assume that it's a recent customer you want to recommend you for your standard product or service.

Then, follow the following guideline dialogue:

You: *"What did you think of the service? Were you happy with it?"*

Your customer: *"Yes, it was good thanks."*

You: *"Great. What did you like best about it?"*

Your customer: *"I really like the Turbo Clean feature. It made it a lot easier to use than other machines we've tried where we've had a lot of problems stopping dirt building up which eventually stops them working and you have to spend 15 minutes cleaning them. Our technicians hate it so the self-cleaning feature was a big help."*

You: *"Thanks. I'm glad you liked it. I'm collecting a few testimonials from customers at the moment. Would it be OK if you helped me out quickly by writing a short testimonial?"*

Your customer: *"Yes, no problem."*

You: *"OK. Thank you. I know you're busy so to make it quicker and easier for you, would it be OK if I took what you just told me and turned it into a quick recommendation. Then you can cut, change, adapt or change it however you like. Would that be OK?"*

Your customer: *"Yes of course."*

Now that you've established what your customer liked most about your product, you can go to Linkedin and request a recommendation in the usual way.

However, this time, rather than letting them write the recommendation, you write the recommendation you want based on what they've told you.

You give them the option of changing it in any way they want AND you include the information that will be of most marketing benefit to you.

All they have to do is copy and paste your recommendation, as if they'd written it themselves.

Because it's quicker and easier for them, most people make zero or only minor changes to what you've suggested and then send you the completed recommendation.

The result is a win-win for both parties.

You help your customer save time and hassle by writing the recommendation for you so that they don't have to take 10 minutes out of their busy day to go online and think of what to say.

And you get a fantastic recommendation that fulfills your marketing requirements AND is completely consistent with what your customers really think about your product.

So there you have it; two quick and easy ways to get more testimonials that will be a huge benefit to your marketing.

Creating a sales document with your recommendations
Once you've built up 10, 20 or more recommendations you can easily turn them into a powerful sales and marketing document.

Simply cut and past the recommendations into a Microsoft Word document, lay them out in a format you're happy with and save them as a PDF.

You can now print or share the document with new prospects. You can also upload it to other websites, including SlideShare.

It's fantastic because it's also highly rated by search engines like Google.

Type your name into Google and – chances are – your recommendations will be one of the first listings.

This creates a great impression when people look online to find out more information about you.

So always be asking for recommendations and turn them into a powerful sales and marketing document you can use and share both on and off line.

You can also upload it to SlideShare to make it easy to share and more likely to appear when prospects Google your name or products.

5. Contact information

If you want potential and existing customers to get in touch with you, it makes sense to make it easy for them, right?

Remember that only people you're connected to will be able to see your contact details if you've entered them in the 'contact details' section.

If you've typed them into your summary, they'll be visible in the public version of your profile that people see if they click through to your Linkedin page from a Google search.

There may be reasons why you don't want everyone you're connected with to have your mobile phone number but at least include the number of your reception desk or PA.

Make sure you include the following contact information in your profile.

Email address – A professional work address, not your angelrobot999@yahoo.com address. It looks unprofessional.

Phone number – Whichever number you want only those people you're connected with to be able to call you on. And if you don't want them to call you, ask yourself why you're connected to them in the first place?

Address – Having a physical address makes you look credible. Would you trust a website with no contact details and no physical location? Again, this will only be visible to people you're connected to.

Linkedin URL – This is the website address for your public Linkedin profile; the one anyone can see whether they're connected to you or not. The default URL is a messy-looking series of numbers. You can customize this to get a much more professional-looking URL to use on external marketing material.

MORNING MOTIVATION

"The pessimist complains about the wind; the optimist expects it to change; the realist adjusts the sail." – **W.A. Ward**

"Your attitude, not aptitude, will determine your altitude."
– **Zig Ziglar**

"Success is the child of audacity." – **Benjamin Disraeli**

"Being a one of a kind means we are automatically the best in the world at what we do." – **Victor Williamson**

"However vast the darkness, we must supply our own light."
– **Stanley Kubrick**

"Each of us is a unique strand in the intricate web of life and here to make a contribution." – **Deepak Chopra**

"The bigger the problem. The bigger the gift it contains."
– **Norman Vincent Peale**

"Do the thing you fear most and the death of fear is certain."
– **Mark Twain**

"The struggle you're in today is developing the strength you need tomorrow." – **Robert Tew**

"Wake up with determination; go to bed with satifaction."
– **George Lorimer**

"You do not believe what you see. You see what you believe."
– **Brian Tracy**

What words of wisdom get you motivated for a great day every morning? Let me know . . . @TomMallens #8AMINSPIRATION

A SECRET THAT MIGHT SHOCK YOU

I'd like to tell you a secret. One that transformed how I think about marketing.

And skyrocketed the results I got in business.

I learnt it from an interesting man called Stefan, who I bumped into at an otherwise pretty forgettable and grey networking event.

It was the secret of writing more persuasively.

So that anyone reading what you write is more likely to read it all. And then, actually do what you ask at the end.

If you can write words that sell effectively, and speak persuasively in front of people too, then you've got a winning combination.

And you tend to sell a lot more in process.

If you sign-up for my emails at
www.tommallens.com/moreleadsfromlinkedin
then you'll learn how to write words that do your selling for you.

And loads of other invaluable stuff too.

Which means you'll make your job easier and get better results as well.

It's free. And it only takes 30 seconds.

Just go to www.tommallens.com/moreleadsfromlinkedin now.

CHAPTER 7

How it pays you to be liked

AN INTERESTING THOUGHT TO HELP YOU SELL MORE

If you understand how something works, it becomes easier to get good at it, right?

Which means that if you understand how sales works, it becomes easier to make more sales.

Here are 6 steps in the sales process:

1. Find and identify prospects
2. Make contact and build rapport
3. Get information
4. Check the facts
5. Make a proposal
6. Ask for the business

Linkedin can help a LOT with the first three steps in this sales process.

I can also help you get better at the other three too.

If you'd like to know exactly how Linkedin can help you make more sales, just drop me a line.

Don't worry, I won't try any high-pressure sales stuff.

It's a quick chat and if it's not right for you, it's zero problem.

But you don't know unless you ask.

**So give me a quick call on +44(0)1926 678 920
or email tom@tommallens.com.**

S o you've become known on Linkedin by connecting with the right people.

And you've built up your likeability with a great profile AND some great content.

But as you're sat there reading this, you might be wondering if it actually helps.

Does being likeable really make a difference? Surely, it's the quality and pricing of your product or service that makes the difference; not simply whether people feel you're the kind of person they like?

Put it this way, if people don't like you in business, your quality and pricing is going to have to be leagues ahead of the competition to overcome the fact that you and your potential customer don't get on.

The same is true on social media.

Being likeable matters. Full stop.

And this is where so many people go wrong – desperately trying to promote their products and services.

Or posting super-bland and boring updates that get a big YAWN rather than getting people heading for the like, share or comment buttons.

There's nothing wrong with selling or promoting your services, but – unless there are special circumstances – it tends not to work.

If you go to a sales meeting, you build up some rapport first.

You ask how business is going. You say you like the painting on their office wall. You throw in some small talk to help build likeability.

So do the same on social media. Be likeable and be true to who you are.

Let's take an example.

For the last year, I've published an inspirational quote on Linkedin at 8am every weekday morning.

In case you're wondering, no, I don't sit at my desk ready to post this information everyday at 8am.

I auto-schedule all the posts in advance. We'll look at why auto-scheduling updates on social media could be a great idea for you and your company in the third and final Be Trusted section of this book.

So why do I post this at 8am everyday? For several reasons! Here are just a few:

- To establish a consistent presence
- To associate myself with the kinds of information I love
- To attract fellow motivation-junkies
- To create engagement with my network

The logic goes as follows (and I'd strongly encourage you to think of your own version to achieve all of the following in your network):

If I only update my status a few times a week, there's a high chance people will miss that update.

The chance to show up when they login to Linkedin is gone.

By scheduling an update at a consistent time every day, people in your network begin to expect (and want) to see you.

That's a powerful thing when those people are potential customers and useful contacts.

Next, I love inspirational quotes. Perhaps you do too?

Posting information that you love on social media is a great way to associate yourself with the kinds of information that you love in real life AND to let your network see what kind of person you really are.

Are you a wise-cracking gag merchant? Then post a daily joke.

Are you a detail-obsessed numbers-junkie? Then post some daily statistical trivia.

Do you LOVE ancient Greek history? Then post a daily fact about one of your favourite ancient gods.

Be true to yourself and the people that like you will quickly let you know with likes, shares and all kinds of online love.

My most popular post was a picture of me at work behind my computer while sat in Temple Bar in Dublin with a pint of Guiness.

I know that everyone who liked it is on my wavelength. They too believe that work should be FUN!

Which makes it all the easier for me to follow-up with these people and arrange warm phone calls and appointments.

Some people might not like gags, numbers or ancient Greece.

And that's fine, you'd have to overcome that rapport barrier anyway.

And it's better to be loved by some customers and not loved by others than it is to be a bland and distant memory in the minds of customers who have forgotten who you are.

As you post likeable content more frequently, you will start to get members of your network liking and sharing your updates.

This is a great opportunity. It's potentially new or repeat customers proactively telling you they like what you're telling them.

And if they like the information you're sharing consistently, they begin to trust you as a person worth speaking to.

It tells you that you have similar tastes as the people that like your information – which is a great foundation for building rapport.

The fact that someone likes your content then gets shared to everyone in their networks too.

It's an exact mirror of word-of-mouth marketing in the off-line world.

The key is to make your updates memorable, with a consistent tagline and a publishing time that's consistent each day.

Without this kind of consistent and memorable information, your activity will be largely wasted. For example:

"Great article in the Harvard Business Review about change management."

… posted once at 11am on a Monday morning is unlikely to be seen or remembered by anyone in your network. However...

"DAVE'S RECOMMENDED READS: Today, it's a great article on 5 things change management consultants can do in the next 5 minutes to win new business."

... posted every day at 1:30pm (with a new recommended read each day) is likely to quickly become remembered as a regular feature of logging in to Linkedin by everyone in Dave's network.

Over a few weeks and months, I noticed many of the same names liking my 8AM INSPIRATION posts.

Among them was a sales manager at a large Birmingham-telecomms company called Steve.

Exactly the kind of person it's useful for me to speak to.

Steve is a fellow motivation-addict so I knew that when I got in touch and mentioned the daily motivational posts he'd know exactly who I was.

Sure enough, we got on instantly.

Creating a consistent presence that reflects who you are and is likeable is super powerful.

And it's one of the biggest missed opportunities most people don't take advantage of.

I was contacted out of the blue one day by Paul, a consultant in the rail industry.

He talked as if we'd met each other before.

Why? Because he'd seen my updates every time he logged on to Linkedin for months which meant a sense of likeability and rapport naturally followed.

Paul is a great contact and happily recommended loads of companies to speak to for the range of aluminium panels we sell at Fibrecore.

I once met the former bouncer, martial arts revolutionary, writer and spiritual pioneer Geoff Thompson.

A picture of Geoff and I on Linkedin attracted dozens of likes and comments and made it easy for me to make contact with all the new contacts that engaged with the picture on the grounds that we were both huge fans of Geoff.

I had instant rapport with everyone who liked, commented or shared the picture.

And the list of people included sales managers, marketers and scores of other ideal prospects.

If you don't know Geoff Thompson, I recommend finding out more about him.

He started life as a young man terrified of spiders, disempowered from sexual abuse and confined to a life of dull factory jobs which he hated.

However, through courageously confronting his demons, he went on to become one of the world's most influential martial arts instructors, a BAFTA-winning screenwriter and best-selling author.

I've lost count of the number of warm phone calls that have sprung off the back of these regular updates through repeated likes and shares.

And the number of people that have told me they look out for that daily hit of inspiration at 8am.

Invariably, these are the kinds of pro-active, go-getting people who like regular doses of inspiration.

Which means they're the kind of people it's MUCH easier for me to build rapport with.

Find the updates that are right for you and you'll attract the kind of people you find it easy to get on with too.

A consistent and authentic presence on Linkedin does wonders for spreading awareness of who you are.

And it magnetically attracts the kinds of people you want to speak to in business, even if you do nothing!

So think about the kinds of update that are authentic, likeable and that you can generate in sufficient quantities to create a daily stream of them.

And when people like, share or comment on your updates, say thank you with a comment of your own.

You wouldn't (I assume) ignore someone that paid you a compliment face-to-face.

So why do it on social media? Make sure you respond and engage everyone that interacts with you online.

That means thanking people who join your network with follow-up messages.

And asking people that want to connect with you why they're getting in touch.

Take an interest in them and ask to find out more about them.

People love the opportunity to talk about themselves.

So asking them to do this on social media is a quick, easy and effective way to do this.

It builds likeability quickly and easily.

The key now is to address the one thing that's missing.

Trust . . .

HAVE YOU SEEN THIS MAN?

Barry Green is wanted for social sales training. Barry is 43 years old. He is a salesman for a technology company in Somerset. Barry spends a lot of time cold-calling He could get more leads more easily and more often if he spent just 3.5 hours learning how to use Linkedin in an effective way, without making the mistakes most salespeople make that stop them getting a steady stream of leads and referrals.

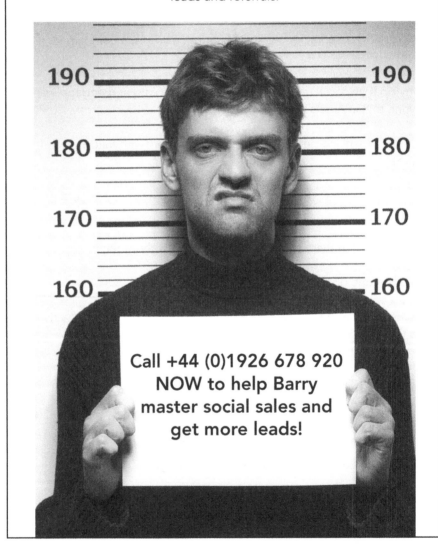

CHAPTER 8

The importance of trust in sales

WIN A CHANCE OF A MYSTERY PRIZE!

If you take a pic of yourself with your copy of
Get Past The Gatekeeper and mention me on Linkedin or Twitter,
then each month, you'll be entered into a prize draw to win a
cool mystery prize.

So get snapping those selfies now!

www.linkedin.com/in/TomMallens
@TomMallens #GetPastTheGatekeeper

Would you do business with someone the first time you met them?

I don't mean the first time you have a face-to-face sit-down meeting with them at their office after meeting them a few weeks ago.

I mean literally the first time you ever lay eyes on them, there and then?

Possibly. It really depends.

Whether you do or you don't, when you've only just met someone and you're in a sales situation, your brain is dealing with a lot of unknown quantities.

On top of thinking about whether you need or want the product, on top of questioning whether the price is right and what the benefits will be, you have one MASSIVE obstacle to tackle.

Trust.

If someone you've never met before tries to sell you something, you brain is on high-alert for danger.

And if in any doubt, it doesn't want to take the risk.

You're worried you'll be swindled, defrauded or make to look stupid.

It's the reason so many people walk straight past clip-boarded charity workers in the street.

Their brains are screaming danger at them and telling them that they're not to be trusted.

Take an opposite example by comparison. Your long-term business contact of 20 years gets in touch and asks to meet up for lunch to talk about some new opportunities.

They might very well deep down be keen on the idea of selling you something.

But you go along to meet them happily.

Why? Because you trust them. And, as a result, your brain has not gone into fear-mode.

Why do you trust them? A big part of the reason is that you've had time to get to know them.

And that comes with consistent, repeated interactions.

You don't need to read many business books to stumble over the following statistics. You might have seen them sometime. They go like this:

- 2% of sales are made on the first contact.
- 3% of sales are made on the second contact.
- 5% of sales are made on the third contact.
- 10% of sales are made on the fourth contact.
- 80% of sales are made on the fifth to twelfth contact.

In other words, the more you speak to people, the more you sell.

And this is where social media like Linkedin works brilliantly. Because it helps you make those first, second, third... or even twelfth contacts more quickly and easily.

Of course, you still have to speak to prospects at some point but every one of your engagements on social media builds trust and moves you closer to the sale.

If you really have read the statistics above, then you've probably also read that most salespeople don't follow up with prospects nearly enough.

They don't build up trust through repeated engagement over time. The figures go like this:

- 48% of sales people never follow up with a prospect.
- 25% of sales people make a second contact and stop.
- 12% of sales people make three contacts and stop.

Only 10% of sales people make more than three contacts with a prospect.

Most of these sales people that don't engage their prospects enough could make giant leaps forward with a decent presence on Linkedin.

One that isn't sporadic and inconsistent. But one that's consistent and persistent!

If you only update your Linkedin status twice a week, then unless someone logs in within a few hours either side of your update, there's a chance that they probably won't see it.

However, if your Linkedin status is updated 4 times every day, then whenever someone logs in, they'll see you on their newsfeed.

And what if, instead of just posting updates in their newsfeed, you're messaging them useful information, liking, sharing and commenting on their updates, starting discussions in the groups they're members of... and more.

Every time they're logged in, they see you; helping them with valuable information, interacting with them and generally being someone who's good at what they do and good at helping other people.

That goes a LONG way to building up trust with the people you want to do business with.

And it quickly means that – in combination with phone calls and face-to-face meetings – you move past the first, second and third contacts to the tenth, eleventh and twelfth.

Which is where you'll find your conversion rates and success start to sky-rocket.

Using Linkedin (and social media in general) to build up trust is really important to your sales efforts.

And it's something that a lot of people forget to do.

Instead, they begin a frenzy of activity on social media for a few hours and then forget about it for a month, followed by another manic episode of updates and messages.

Developing a few habits that make social media engagement part of your regular routine is the key to being consistent and building that all-important trust with your prospects.

It also serves another important function. It has you ready on people's radars when they're ready to buy.

Imagine something you bought in the last week. Anything. It doesn't matter.

Did you want to buy it the week before, a month before or even a year before?

Probably not. There comes a point in time when you (or anyone else) is ready to buy.

And therefore, there comes a point when they decide who to consider buying from and, in turn, who to actually buy from.

If you can be on your prospect's mind when they decide who to consider buying from, you will – all other things being equal – have a higher chance of getting meetings, phone calls and sales opportunities.

Being on social media gives you a powerful way to be on people's minds when they're considering who to buy from.

Not just because they see you when they log on to Linkedin. But because you can achieve powerful marketing and branding objectives and build strong social ties that get you remembered quickly and easily on B2B social media like Linkedin.

LEADS

The identification of a person or entity that has the interest, authority and budget (i.e. money) to purchase a product or service.

ARE YOU IN SALES?

Do you get frustrated when your calls aren't put through to key decision-makers?

Or do you wish more clients would come to you – instead of you chasing them?

If so, you can get 37 tried and tested ways to win more business-to-business sales leads in my exclusive free report.

Tips 5, 12 and 29 will help most salespeople ditch awkward cold calls AND get more in-bound leads more quickly and easily than ever.

They're the same tips that landed sales and marketing manager Hana Smiddy £60,000 of new business opportunities within days.

So don't miss out, download your copy now at:

www.tommallens.com/moreleadsfromlinkedin

CHAPTER 9

How to establish trust on social media

WHAT WORKS BEST FOR YOU IN SALES?

Do you have hints or tips that help you beat gatekeepers?

Or specific questions about anything in this book?

Drop me a line on Linkedin or Twitter

And I'll do my best to answer!

www.linkedin.com/in/TomMallens
@TomMallens #GetPastTheGatekeeper

f someone trusts you, they're more likely to want to do business with you.

By updating your Linkedin status regularly you can stay in contact with your business contacts and generate engagement and conversations with them.

Most importantly, this kind of regular presence generates trust.

If people like your content once, they might forget about you after a day or two.

If you're on Linkedin every time they log in, you quickly start to generate familiarity and they'll start to trust you as an expert in your field.

It's a good window of opportunity to stay present in your prospects' thoughts.

As we've discussed, many people update their status on Linkedin sporadically with an article they've read.

If their potential customers don't log-in on that day, they won't see the update. The opportunity for engagement is lost.

So how can you publish regular status updates without logging in every single day?

Using a social media management tool is one simple and effective way to do that.

The best ones will let you pre-schedule the publication of content days, weeks or even months in advance.

It means that whenever people log into Linkedin, you'll be there on their radar.

And when the time is right for them to buy, you'll be among the first people they think to contact.

Most social media management tools can do a lot of other useful things; from listening to what customers are saying about your industry or company to automating social media marketing campaigns.

There are no hard and fast rules for when and how often to post on Linkedin. But three key factors to take account of are:

- **Content** – What will you post that generates conversations and engagement with customers?

- **Time** – When are the best times to post that most people will see?

- **Frequency** – How often should you post to maximise the chances of being seen?

Most people log on to Linkedin first thing in the morning, at lunchtime and after work. Sunday evening is also a surprisingly good time.

Many people take a moment to look through emails and check their Linkedin accounts on Sundays as they prepare for the week ahead.

So think about scheduling updates for these times (mornings, lunchtimes, after work and Sunday evenings).

Updating your Twitter status 20 times a day is not at all uncommon. On Linkedin however, that kind of frequency might not be appropriate. Three or four times is fine. The important thing is consistency.

You know how people used to look up names of prospects in the phone book... and then actually ring and try and speak to them?

This seems to have gone out of fashion among some people since the advent of social media.

And it's a shame because it prevents most people getting the best out of Linkedin and social media.

I've had numerous people send me supposedly 'urgent' messages on Linkedin and Twitter, expecting an immediate response.

They seemed to forget that I might not actually be on social media 24 hours a day.

If you want a quick response, give someone a call! Sure, send them an email, Linkeidn message and tweet too but don't rely on this exclusively.

They call it a marketing mix for a reason – it's supposed to be a mix of different things!

As a salesperson you have all these social media communication tools at hand to help you achieve your objectives.

So it seems crazy to stick rigidly to only one at the exclusion of all others.

They're tools. And like a hammer, spade or screwdriver, you need to select the right one for the job.

Some people have become so fixated on social media they forget about the telephone and face-to-face meetings entirely.

This problem works in reverse too. I've met loads of seasoned salespeople who refuse to try and learn news skills or use new technologies.

In part, they complain that social media doesn't do what the telephone call or face-to-face meeting does.

That's fine. It's not meant to. A hammer doesn't dig a hole. A spade doesn't turn a screw.

You need to use the tools available to you for the job they were meant to do.

If you want to turn online engagement, rapport and in-bound leads into sales, you still have to speak to people and get in front of them.

Social media has not changed that. And I doubt it ever will.

But social media has given you MASSIVELY powerful new ways to build relationships, attract in-bound leads and find new business opportunities more easily and more often.

Often, it's before and after a phone call or face-to-face meeting where social media can be so powerful.

Use social media ineffectively and people won't know who you are. In this case, you may as well just make a cold call.

> Use social media effectively and prospects will know who you are before your call and be happy to speak to you.

Below is a simple way to take Linkedin interactions offline and have more productive conversations with potential customers.

Taking conversations offline and speaking to people on the phone or face-to-face is one of the best ways to build trust.

Here's a simple sequence of actions you can use to build trust and successfully get prospects on the phone.

Find people you'd like to speak to
Linkedin groups are great for finding people you want to speak to.

Groups are natural segmentations of the Linkedin networking community according to subjects of shared interest.

There are millions of groups covering everything from spirituality to supply chain management.

So whatever sector you work in, you can find a group packed with people you have something in common with and who will make ideal potential customers or strategic referral partners.

People often make the mistake of joining groups full of people offering similar products and services to them, instead of finding groups full of potential customers.

Don't make this mistake as it will severely limit your opportunities to get in-bound leads.

Send them a message asking for permission to connect

Now that you're in a Linkedin group, you could just start inviting people in the group to connect with you.

But if people don't know you, they may wonder why you're so keen to get in touch.

A much more effective approach is to send people a message explaining why you'd like to get in touch.

At the end of the message, ask for permission to send them an invitation to connect.

This soft and polite approach almost always gets a response, especially when it's combined with an offer to help them in some way and an explanation of how you could do this.

The reason this is good is that it gets people looking at your profile and finding out about who you are and what you do.

If you've created a perfect Linkedin profile to start with, it will immediately spark people's interest and build rapport before the call has even started.

Send them an invitation to connect

In the vast majority of cases, you'll get a quick message back from people saying that they're happy for you to connect.

In which case, you can send a Linkedin connection request as normal. And you can indicate how you know the person you're trying to connect with; in this case, through the group.

The fact that you're both in the same group is a great rapport builder.

Within a day or two, you will get a notification that they've accepted your connection request.

The key point here is that you've had 2 or 3 interactions with the potential customer in which you've offered to help.

And those interactions will be building rapport all the while.

As soon as you've connected with a new contact on Linkedin, you'll be able to see their email address and other contact information.

You even get the option to download all your contacts' email addresses, which is a great way to quickly gain a powerful database for email marketing.

Pick up the telephone
This one is fairly self-explanatory. Most people's profiles list their preferred telephone number.

If there's no telephone number, you can either message your new contact to ask when is a good time to call or get in touch via the contact details on their company website.

I've found it very helpful to remind the person early on in the call that you connected recently on Linkedin and that you always try to speak to people in your network.

After all, what's the point of connecting with people that you don't want to talk to and try to help out?

It's a logic that makes sense to people and gets phone calls off to a productive start.

From there, it's down to your telephone skills to take the conversation forward in a way that's most appropriate.

I've found the key to success from this approach is a strict process-driven approach.

A regular half-hour slot in which you work through contacting all your new Linkedin connections by phone is a great place to start.

Many people make the mistake of forgetting that when it comes to business, social media is just one part of the marketing mix.

It's a powerful, revolutionary and effective one. But it works best when it's used in combination with other marketing tools too.

> One of the big reasons some people don't get results from social media is that fact that while their social media activity may be good, the rest of their marketing sucks!

It can be painful to admit but I've seen numerous examples where it's true.

They typically have loads of great social activity online but a weak and inconsistent brand, a poorly defined and unexciting offer and too few marketing channels to get the message to the right people.

You might be familiar with the idea that more sales get made on the fifth, sixth and seventh contact with the customer than on the first or second.

The problem is that most B2B salespeople give up after the first or second contact with the customer in which they express indifference or don't bite your hand off to try your services.

A great way to use Linkedin is to add interactions with your prospect into the total and turn one or two contacts into five, six or seven points.

For example, if you find an interesting potential customer on Linkedin, perhaps using the advanced search or in a group, think about the following steps:

1. Connect on Linkedin – As described earlier in the book, this is your chance to establish rapport and add value thanks to the information in the prospects' profile.

2. Follow-up with a phone call – Get in touch to explain that based on their Linkedin information, there could be some interesting opportunities to discuss.

3. Get agreement to send a letter – Use the call to get permission to send a letter, then create a great piece of direct mail with an attention-grabbing headline, compelling offer and call to action PLUS loads of rapport-building information garnered from Linkedin.

4. Send a Linkedin message following-up your letter – This could be a private message or they could now be included in a marketing-focused message as part of one of your tags on Linkedin. This could be a good time to give them a name-check in a status update, like some of their content or (even better) make a couple of targeted introductions to potentially useful contacts – showing your ability and willingness to help them.

5. Email a YouTube video – Few things add the personal touch to a message than a video. If you can't be there in person to deliver the message, a video let's you establish rapport more quickly and easily.

6. Call back to get their reaction – At this stage, if you've got this right, your main objective is to simply decide how it's easiest for them to pay. If you've identified them well on Linkedin and got the right information into your marketing material, they should be all set to buy.

This longer-term outlook with more contact between you and the potential customer builds trust, especially if you can help or add value to the prospect in some way at every stage.

If you wouldn't relentlessly try to sell to someone in person, then don't use social media to do that either.

Take an approach that's right for you and your industry.

Use Linkedin to gather valuable information that will help build rapport and trust at every stage of the process, in your social media, your direct mail, your emails and your phone calls.

When and what to say on the phone
So what should you say to people on the phone when you do get in touch? And when should you call?

Mastering the ability to make effective phone calls is a vital business skill and it's one that will make your lead-finding on social media much more effective.

By setting up phone calls on Linkedin, you'll be able to fill your diary with warm opportunities to speak to prospects.

But those phone calls will go much more smoothly if you're effectively using the phone as a tool to get the results you want.

As mentioned, it's best to call prospects within 48-hours of some kind of engagement on Linkedin. These times include:

- After accepting a connection request
- After a discussion in a group
- After a repeated exchange of messages
- After regular likes, shares or comments on your updates

All these types of interaction give you an opportunity for warm phone calls, rather than those awkward and frustrating cold ones.

In a study at a California-based call centre, tele-marketers made more than 1,000 cold calls to senior managers asking for a face-to-face appointment. They used a standard cold calling script and measured their results.

They then repeated the process but added the line: "I understand we're in the same group on Linkedin."

The number of appointments they booked went up by more than 70%. That's a MASSIVE difference from just a small tweak.

The reason for this improvement is significant. Suddenly, the prospect sees that you're not a typical cold caller who has no interest in them and is merely ploughing through a script.

That small piece of information (that you're in the same group on Linkedin) shows the prospect that you have shared interests, that you are genuinely interested in them and that you have taken the time to do some research. It shows that you care.

And that will have a HUGE impact on the results of your cold calling.

I remember calling Paul, the director of a recruitment firm, shortly after we connected on Linkedin.

I reminded him that we'd recently made contact on Linkedin and that I was calling to quickly see if and how I could help – something I like to do with as many new contacts as possible.

Paul remembered that call and more than a year later, he rang to book a training session for his team on how they could use Linkedin more effectively.

So what can you say to maximise the effectiveness of your calls to new contacts on Linkedin?

Here's a guide to the key phrases that will help you get results.

Calling prospects to build your network

One of the best ways to build your personal brand and create a powerful network of engaged contacts is to speak to them and add value when you do.

One of the best times to do this is shortly after you have connected on Linkedin.

After you've connected and sent them some useful information, you can ring them up – ideally within 24 to 48 hours – and open the conversation with the following:

"Hi. I'm just calling because we connected on Linkedin recently. I always try to speak to people in my network. I wanted to find out a bit more about you and see if and how I could help moving forward. If we don't ever speak, there doesn't seem much point being connected. Does that make sense?"

Using these words does a number of important things.

1. Eliminates cold call fear

It reminds the person that you've connected on Linkedin and that they have, in that sense, opted-in to a relationship with you.

It tells them that this is a personal and well-researched call that is worth taking, rather than a cold and impersonal one.

---

2. Puts prospects at ease
It lets the person know that you ALWAYS try to speak to people in your network.

This is a normal thing that you do. You're not trying to sell them anything.

Using the words *'I always try to speak to people in my network'* reassures people that this isn't a sales call and makes them feel safer and more comfortable talking to you.

3. Builds rapport quickly and easily
By explaining that you 'wanted to find out a bit more about you', you give people the opportunity to do their favourite thing – talk about themselves.

Most people start cold calls by telling their prospect all about themselves and their products. In reality – as mentioned several times in this book – people are only interested in themselves.

Explaining that you want to know more about someone makes them feel good, feel secure and feel like this is NOT your usual sales call.

4. Gets them saying yes
When you remind people that there doesn't seem much point being connected if you don't ever speak to them, you give them a statement that is very hard for them to disagree with. In fact, I've never had anyone disagree with this statement.

Everytime I use those words, they say yes. Which is extremely important in psychological terms for building trust.

Once people start saying yes to you, it becomes much easier for them to keep saying yes.

If they've said yes to speaking to you, they're much more likely to say 'yes' to a face-to-face appointment with you; as the results of the call centre study in Florida pove.

Once you've built up some rapport and overcome their fear of the cold call, you can take things to the next level by dropping in some more rapport-building information from Linkedin itself.

As mentioned in the first section of this book, Linkedin tells you who you know that prospects already know too.

So you can follow your opening statement with:

"I just noticed that we're both in the (XYZ) group and we both know (John Smith) too."

Whether you use this phrase in messages within Linkedin or on the phone, the results are the same:

- More rapport
- More trust
- More results!

As we've seen from the research into weak ties by Mark Granovetter, there are powerful psychological reasons why this information about mutual contacts and shared groups is so important.

Make sure you keep an eye out for it.

Have a plan
One of the best ways to getting better results from phone calls is to have an objective. If you don't have an objective, you can't achieve it.

Generally speaking, I have two potential objectives when I call a prospect I've found on Linkedin:

1. Add value to help build my network of useful and engaged contacts.

Or

2. Get a face-to-face appointment.

In some cases, if I'm aiming to get a face-to-face appointment, I'll switch to objective 1 mid-way through.

At Fibrecore, we sell products with fairly complex application criteria. Sometimes, during a chat with a prospect it becomes clear that they are not actually a potential customer.

Perhaps they don't have the equipment needed to process our raw materials or perhaps their manufacturing processes mean they couldn't use our machinery.

If that's the case, I may decide to simply revert to objective number 1.

In both cases, you can't have a successful sales call if you don't have an objective.

Ask yourself what your objectives are when you call new or existing contacts on Linkedin and focus on getting the outcomes that are right for you.

I spent so long making unproductive cold calls before I discovered Linkedin.

With some good cold call skills combined with the power of Linkedin, you're on a fast track to beating more gatekeepers than ever before.

Here are 10 golden rules I learnt (often the hard way) that made a HUGE difference to my sales call success. If you practice them, they will do exactly the same for you:

1. Look up your prospects on Linkedin
Nothing flatters prospects more than when you know about them BEFORE you call. It shows you're professional and trustworthy.

Best of all, it only takes a second. Log onto Linkedin, use the standard or advanced search, and see what useful information you can get about your prospect.

As mentioned previously, look for the names of mutual contacts, the names of groups you're both in, and any interesting details about the person you want to speak to. This includes:

- Mutual contacts you both know
- Groups you're both in
- Shared professional history
- Schools or universities you went to
- Likes and dislikes
- Hobbies and recreational interests
- Charitable causes and organisations they support

Linkedin is a great source of this kind of information which will fill you with confidence and get your calls off to a great start.

2. Have an objective
As mentioned, this is essential to getting results. Whatever your objective for the call, focus on using it to take you at least one step closer to making your prospect a customer.

If you make the call and don't get an appointment but you get the name of a new contact or other bit of useful information, then that call was worth making.

The person, or company, you called is now one step closer to becoming a customer.

Remind yourself that you're making excellent progress and keep going!

3. Smile
Smiling before you make sales calls does several vital things. It puts you in a positive frame of mind and it makes you sound more friendly and approachable – which makes prospects more interested in speaking to you.

4. Make the call about them
People love to talk about themselves. So one of the best ways to get people engaged in your sales calls is to ask them about them, their products, processes and priorities.

Phrases such as 'how could I help best?' and 'could you tell me a little bit more about yourself' are great ways to get people talking.

5. Be confident
Confidence is what will power you through the awkward calls. It's what will give you the strength to ask that extra question that gives you the information you need.

Confidence is infectious too. If you confidently ask questions, people are more likely to give you the answers you want.

It's important not to qualify your questions with phrases such as 'can I ask a cheeky question' or 'would you mind if I asked who your suppliers are'.

Instead, clearly, confidently and calmly ask what you want to know. Let your prospects decide if they want to tell you – you'll be surprised how often they do.

If you ask timidly, you'll get a timid response. So be confident and ask questions like the answers you want are no big deal.

Very often, this attitude will rub off onto your prospect and they'll respond like the information you want is no big deal too.

6. Mention your shared interests
As mentioned, explaining briefly that you have things in common with your prospect is an extremely important way to build rapport.

And if you're in B2B sales, Linkedin is the best place to get this information.

7. Develop a winning mindset
If you make sales calls, you will get rejections. It's frustrating, demoralising and tiring.

If you're not careful, you can get fed up and convince yourself it's a good idea to stop.

Instead, remember that every rejection is taking you one step closer to success. Every rejection is giving you the information, experience and know-how to become a better salesman.

If you think about how the calls went and look to improve every time, then every rejection or failure to achieve your objective becomes a valuable lesson – one that you can be genuinely grateful for.

In the words of the Brazilian jiu-jitsu master Carlos Gracie: "There is no losing. You either win, or you learn."

When it comes to sales calls, you either achieve your objective, or you learn how to achieve your objective next time.

8. Whatever you do, call!
The biggest mistake you can make is talking yourself out of the need to make calls.

Making sales calls gets results.

If you make zero calls, you will get zero results.

It's so easy to convince yourself that you can put off the sales calls you want to make until tomorrow.

Unfortunately, when tomorrow comes, you'll tell yourself you can put them off to tomorrow again.

I found details of a food packaging company on Linkedin and used the information to find and speak to the right people about Fibrecore's range of adhesives.

I remember not being in a very productive frame of mind at the time. I was tired and fed-up with a few challenges I was dealing with at the time.

Nevertheless, I got the head of R&D on the phone and things rapidly started to go badly.

The man in question had a PhD in chemistry. I do not! And he assumed that I would understand his company's products at the same level of microscopic detail as he did.

As it quickly became obvious that I didn't, he started to get more and more annoyed that I couldn't answer his questions.

The call ended with me worrying that I had blown the chance to make a good impression and convince the head of R&D that we were a company worth speaking to.

I followed up and followed up, leaving messages and asking for more details about their manufacturing processes.

About 4 months later, that same man met some colleagues at a trade exhibition and berated them (semi-seriously) about how often I'd been calling.

About 8 months later, they started buying from us. Persistence paid off.

If I'd never made that initial call, on a day when making sales calls was the last thing I wanted to do, they would never have started buying.

So whatever you do on Linkedin, make sure you maximise its impact by picking up the phone too.

Look for those interactions and rapport-building pieces of information that will take you past gatekeepers and straight to the decision makers and get calling!

LEADS

1. **Find the right people.**

2. **Give them a compelling offer.**

3. **And a reason to act . . . NOW!**

WIN A CHANCE OF A MYSTERY PRIZE!

If you take a pic of yourself with your copy of
Get Past The Gatekeeper and mention me on Linkedin or Twitter,
then each month, you'll be entered into a prize draw to win a
cool mystery prize.

So get snapping those selfies now!

www.linkedin.com/in/TomMallens
@TomMallens #GetPastTheGatekeeper

CHAPTER 10

Real examples of the benefits you'll get

A SECRET THAT MIGHT SHOCK YOU

I'd like to tell you a secret. One that transformed how I think about marketing.

And skyrocketed the results I got in business.

I learnt it from an interesting man called Stefan, who I bumped into at an otherwise pretty forgettable and grey networking event.

It was the secret of writing more persuasively.

So that anyone reading what you write is more likely to read it all. And then, actually do what you ask at the end.

If you can write words that sell effectively, and speak persuasively in front of people too, then you've got a winning combination.

And you tend to sell a lot more in process.

If you sign-up for my emails at
www.tommallens.com/moreleadsfromlinkedin
then you'll learn how to write words that do your selling for you.

And loads of other invaluable stuff too.

Which means you'll make your job easier and get better results as well.

It's free. And it only takes 30 seconds.

Just go to www.tommallens.com/moreleadsfromlinkedin now.

There are so many ways to use social media to help get the results that are right for you in your business.

But time and time and again, it comes down to those three simple things:

- Be known
- Be liked
- Be trusted

Exactly how you establish them can vary but you must achieve each one to start making more sales and getting the results you want.

Here's how a handful of recent customers have been using Linkedin in different ways to get ahead in their businesses.

The being known strategy

Joan is a Midlands-based food safety specialist. She trains restaurant and catering staff in food hygiene practices.

Joan focused primarily on using Linkedin to find potential customers using the advanced search function and booking face-to-face appointments at the earliest opportunity.

This is all about being known. Joan focused on leveraging Linkedin to show her the people she needed to speak to and give her the background info she needed to make more productive cold calls.

"I quickly made contact with a man who I thought would welcome some training for his business and followed up to get an appointment," said Joan.

"This man not only organised large corporate events but in his private life he sat on the board at a local sheltered housing scheme.

"I was asked to deliver training at 3 of their West Midland centres, to both staff and tenants.

"This would never have happened had I not used Tom's LinkedIn training strategy to make the face-to-face appointments and have the confidence to carry it through.

"As a direct result of that meeting, it became apparent that there was also a need for nutrition and hydration training for his client group.

"So this opened up another opportunity for me and another string to my bow."

While many people connect indiscriminately with people on Linkedin without a strategy or game-plan, Joan got great results by using the 3 easy steps I teach to get more rapport-filled phone calls and meetings more easily and more often.

Most importantly, she ensured she built up recognition and rapport online before picking up the phone and speaking to her prospects.

The being liked strategy

A contact of mine, Nick, is a leading authority on leadership and management development and is also a big fan of social media for B2B sales.

Nick uses a super-effective system on Linkedin built around an irresistible offer for his potential customers.

Nick helps the top managers and leaders in SMEs and large corporations perform more effectively on a day-to-day basis through better time management, goal-setting, decision-making, leadership and more.

Before he started using Linkedin, Nick, like most people in B2B sales, relied on face-to-face networking and a little bit of direct mail to search for leads and sales opportunities.

"It was reasonably effective but not sensational," said Nick.

Like more than 16 million other business people in the UK, Nick signed up with Linkedin around 5 years ago.

"I was good at getting recommendations so I got a lot of online credibility but I wasn't getting a lot of new business."

Nick sells high-value training and has a special offer for potential customers.

Send one person from the organization to one of his courses completely free.

After the first person, other people from the same company pay full rate. But by then, the relationship is already formed thanks to that compelling offer.

In other words, Nick's strategy is all about being liked by his potential customers. They like (in fact, they love) the idea of special-offer free training from one of the country's top names in leadership training.

Today, Linkedin is one of Nick's most effective tools for finding leads and starting conversations with potential customers.

These are Nick's 5 steps to doing business with large companies on Linkedin.

1. Define the characteristics of your ideal contacts
Ask yourself exactly what kind of senior decision makers you want to speak to. Make a mental note of their characteristics, including their job titles and location.

2. Use the advanced search to find prospects
By using this function on Linkedin, you can search for prospects according to keywords in their profile, job title and their location.

3. Choose how to get in touch
Once you've run an advanced search you should see a list of potential prospects. Look through this list and decide who your most likely prospects

are. Don't forget to search for rapport-building information from their profiles.

4. Develop a compelling offer with which to introduce yourself

When you send a message or connection request, it's important to do two things says Nick:

- Build rapport
- Make a compelling offer

Nick takes the time to tweak and personalize his messages and has developed the compelling offer of completely free places to attract interest – rather than just trying to sell immediately to his prospects.

5. Build the communication and follow-up

Ultimately, no-one will send you their credit card details over Linkedin so, at some stage, you have to take your conversation offline.

"I made contact with one HR manager and started a conversation before meeting up for coffee," explains Nick.

"We now have a contract for training 90+ managers worth more than £100,000 over two years.

"I just need a few of the conversations I start with HR managers to come through and I can have a very successful month or year.

"Linkedin has enabled me to win business with the right size of customers. In a very real way, it's feeding my kids."

Sending one message to one potential customer will give you once chance at starting a conversations with a prospect.

But don't forget that sending 20 messages will give you 20 chances. Send 20 messages a week and you've got 1,040 chances every year.

One of the keys to Nick's success has been developing a habit of once a week searching and making contact with new prospects in a focused 30-minute burst of activity.

"It was no more than half an hour's work per week. Now that it's become a routine it's almost a case of copy and pasting. It's easy and very simple to do.

"I've been able to very effectively build relationships with people at the right level of a company and in a relatively small amount of time.

"I now have a system that I can keep repeating and I know will win me business," added Nick.

The being trusted strategy

Gill works as a translator, translating business and legal documents from German to English and vice versa, when she decided to start her own business.

Her business is in the rapidly-growing world of post-editing machine translation.

She supplies companies with post editors; translators trained to check and edit transcripts already translated by machine.

These are as opposed to people who translate text in the traditional method from scratch.

Gill's business was to find post-editors and put them in contact with companies who needed their services.

Post-editing machine translation is still regarded with suspicion by some in the translation industry.

So Gill's strategy to get business from Linkedin was all about winning trust.

She established a consistent presence by auto-publishing her blog on rotation and began growing her network with key influencers and leading figures in the translation industry.

Before long, Gill had contact from someone requiring post-editing machine translators – in other words, her first customer!

It was a day or two later that I received the following text message:

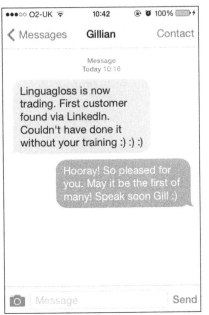

These examples illustrate just a handful of the different ways you can use B2B social media platforms like Linkedin to become better known, liked and trusted by potential customers and, ultimately, do business with them.

MORNING MOTIVATION

"Everything you've ever wanted is on the other side of fear."
– **George Addair**

"The hero & the coward feel the same fear. But the hero uses his fear & projects it onto his opponent." – **Cus D'Amato**

"I would rather die of passion than of boredom." – **Vincent van Gogh**

"People react to criticism in different ways. And my way is to come out fighting." – **David Beckham**

"I can accept failure. Everyone fails at something. But I can't accept not trying." – **Michael Jordan**

"All our dreams can come true if we have the courage to pursue them." – **Walt Disney**

"The greater danger for most of us lies not in setting our aim too high and falling short; but in setting our aim too low and achieving our mark." – **Michelangelo**

"Rejoice in the way things are. When you realise there is nothing lacking, the whole world belongs to you." – **Lao Tzu**

"There is no passion to be found playing small, in settling for a life that is less than the one you are capable of living." – **Nelson Mandela**

"You can never cross the ocean unless you have the courage to lose sight of the shore." – **Christopher Columbus**

What words of wisdom get you motivated for a great day every morning? Let me know . . . @TomMallens #8AMINSPIRATION

AN INTERESTING THOUGHT TO HELP YOU SELL MORE

If you understand how something works, it becomes easier to get good at it, right?

Which means that if you understand how sales works, it becomes easier to make more sales.

Here are 6 steps in the sales process:

1. Find and identify prospects
2. Make contact and build rapport
3. Get information
4. Check the facts
5. Make a proposal
6. Ask for the business

Linkedin can help a LOT with the first three steps in this sales process.

I can also help you get better at the other three too.

If you'd like to know exactly how Linkedin can help you make more sales, just drop me a line.

Don't worry, I won't try any high-pressure sales stuff.

It's a quick chat and if it's not right for you, it's zero problem.

But you don't know unless you ask.

**So give me a quick call on +44(0)1926 678 920
or email tom@tommallens.com.**

CHAPTER 11

How to put it all into practice

WIN A CHANCE OF A MYSTERY PRIZE!

If you take a pic of yourself with your copy of
Get Past The Gatekeeper and mention me on Linkedin or Twitter,
then each month, you'll be entered into a prize draw to win a
cool mystery prize.

So get snapping those selfies now!

www.linkedin.com/in/TomMallens
@TomMallens #GetPastTheGatekeeper

So there you have it. Whatever other ideas this book has given you, I hope it has demystified B2B social media and social selling for you.

A lot of nonsense gets talked about social media but, when you boil it all down, it's nothing more than a tool for doing what people in business have always done: socialise.

Whether you do it face-to-face or online, socializing in a business-to-business context is all about become better known, better liked and better trusted by the people that matter to you most.

Those people might be potential customers but they could also be business allies. referral partners or influential leaders within your industry.

There are a few important points to remember.

The effectiveness of your social media is only as effective as your marketing in general.

If your marketing is terrible, social media will not be as effective.

In fact, there's the risk it will achieve nothing more than a lot of online noise and an ever-growing to-do list.

To ensure your social media is effective, you MUST have an objective that makes sense in business terms.

Whether that's to line-up warm phone calls with new potential customers or to increase customer retention; if you do not have an objective, you make it impossible to achieve it.

So set a primary objective. Ask yourself what the single most important business issue facing your company is right now and consider how using social media as part of your marketing could help.

From there, build your social media on a firm foundation of content that's loaded with your brand identity.

Remember that marketing pyramid we discussed at the beginning of the book again.

Here's a point-by-point summary starting from the top and working down to the foundation – the most important part of all.

Your social media – What's the style of your socialising? What language will you use? How often will you log in and proactively manage your network?

Your content – What will you share with potential customers that gives them an understanding of what it would be like to buy from you?

Your delivery – Is the infrastructure you're using to deliver your message to customers doing the job? When it comes to social media, this is about asking which platforms are right for you.

Your offer – Can you sum your offer up clearly and concisely? If it can't be written down in an exciting and interesting way in a social media status update, there's pretty much no hope of communicating that message effectively to customers.

Your brand – This is THE most important thing to get right because every aspect of your marketing is built on this. If you don't have a consistent brand based around emotions you want your market to associate with you, then you're shooting yourself in the foot before you've even started the race. Basically, you're screwed.

Some people worry about what to say or post on social media.

But I've rarely met people that worry so much about what to say to people they meet in business.

Go to a meeting, exhibition or event and you introduce yourself, ask questions about the other person, share stories about what you do and what you've been up to lately.

Whether you do that online or face-to-face is a secondary consideration.

People that are successful networkers get busy meeting people, learning about them, putting them in contact with useful contacts and talking with passion and excitement about what they do – always looking for a way to use their skills to assist others.

They don't sit there for hours agonizing over whether someone will like them; over whether someone will agree with what they say.

They get out there and make things happen.

Social media is a powerful way to add fuel to that word-of-mouth marketing fire.

And rather than spreading awareness of what you do one person at a time, social media lets you do that on a one-to-many basis.

If, every time they log in to Linkedin people see you, you are MUCH more likely to be the person that's on their mind when they decide who to contact and buy from.

And that goes double if you're the person publishing content they like, offering to help, keeping in touch with useful advice, and generally being sociable – rather than bland, boring and just like everyone else.

WHAT WORKS BEST FOR YOU IN SALES?

Do you have hints or tips that help you beat gatekeepers?

Or specific questions about anything in this book?

Drop me a line on Linkedin or Twitter

And I'll do my best to answer!

www.linkedin.com/in/TomMallens
@TomMallens #GetPastTheGatekeeper

CHAPTER 12

What to go and do NOW!

WANT TO GET MORE SALES LEADS?

There's one surprising thing you can do that will improve your sales results.

It's completely free.

It works on anyone.

And you can use it any time to improve your results.

People do business with people they like.

And what's the easiest way to make more people take a liking to you?

Smile!

The more you smile, the happier people feel around you.

And the happier people feel, the more likely they are to want to work with you.

Give it a try today!

Congratulations on making it to the end of this book!

But remember, in the words of the great Dale Carnegie: "Knowledge is not power until it is applied".

If you don't go away and DO something after reading this book, the results you get will be limited, at best.

It's only be taking action that you will start to get results, including:

- More inbound leads
- More warm (rather than cold) phone calls
- More business opportunities

Whenever you read a new book, it can seem like there's too much information to put into practice and, overwhelmed by decisions, you end up doing nothing.

So, to help you move forward and get results, I've made a brief list of the key actions you should go and put into practice now (in the order that most people find most useful).

Here goes...

1. Spend 10 minutes planning

Answer the following questions (and write down your answers).

A. What is your number 1 business objective you want to help achieve on social media?

More leads? More referrals? More repeat business?

B. What are the key emotions you want people to feel when they think about you?

More happy and entertained? More successful? More financially secure? Or something else . . .?

2. Create your perfect profile

Log onto Linkedin and start to update your profile so it reflects your overall sales objectives and your personal brand.

Make sure you cover the following key areas:

A. Your photograph

Does this reflect who you are?

B. Your professional headline

Does this quickly and effectively sum-up what you do and communicate a benefit you deliver that your ideal customer will understand?

C. Your summary

Use the 6P structure to explain the problems your customer faces and how you can solve them. In particular, remember:

Position - Explain who your customers are and the situation they're in. The more specific you can be, the better. This shows you understand their world and establishes your credibility.

Problem - Remind your customers of a particular problem they have (one that you can solve).

Projection - Describe how bad things will get if they don't do something to tackle the problem.

Proposal - Outline your solution to the problem, how it is delivered and how it eliminates the problem once and for all.

Proof - Give some evidence that your solution really works.

Please - Include a call to action, asking potential customers to get in touch or take some other action.

D. Your recommendations

If you haven't already, start to ask for these from customers, colleagues and anyone else that's appropriate.

E. Your contact details

Make sure it's easy for people to get in contact with you.

3. Decide on updates and information to share

A. Choose a regular type of hint, tip or update you can auto-schedule in advance so that you're always visible whenever anyone in your network logs in to Linkedin.

Make sure this is consistent with your personal brand and the emotions you want people to associate with you.

B. Use your mobile phone to update your Linkedin status with moments, ideas and images from your life that reinforce your personal brand.

4. Always be building your network

Find, get in touch with and socialise with the following types of people:

A. Existing contacts from the past and people you meet now

B. Look for new potential customers, referral partners or industry influencers using:

- Groups
- Advanced search

5. Take your conversations offline

Always look for opportunities to add value to your network. When the time is right, pick up the phone and get talking:

Remember the key phrases:

"I just noticed your profile as we're both in the [XYZ] group . . ."

"I always like to speak to people in my network, otherwise there doesn't seem to be much point being connected. Does that make sense?"

And of course, don't forget to find and connect with me for more information on how you can get more leads from social media in 3 easy steps!

www.linkedin.com/in/TomMallens
@TomMallens
www.youtube.com/TomMallens
www.facebook.com/TomMallens
www.tommallens.com/moreleadsfromlinkedin

CHAPTER 13

What people think of my social sales training

ARE YOU IN SALES?

Do you get frustrated when your calls aren't put through to key decision-makers?

Or do you wish more clients would come to you – instead of you chasing them?

If so, you can get 37 tried and tested ways to win more business-to-business sales leads in my exclusive free report.

Tips 5, 12 and 29 will help most salespeople ditch awkward cold calls AND get more in-bound leads more quickly and easily than ever.

They're the same tips that landed sales and marketing manager Hana Smiddy £60,000 of new business opportunities within days.

So don't miss out, download your copy now at:

www.tommallens.com/moreleadsfromlinkedin

f you're sat there reading this book and wondering whether social media can really work for you and your organisation, take a look at what a few recent customers think.

Then, to find out how you could get more leads from Linkedin more easily and more often in 3 easy steps, simply call Tom Mallens at Social Innovation Media Ltd on +44 (0)1926 678 920, email tom@tommallens.com or tweet @TomMallens.

"Tom's course was fun, informative and packed with excellent information on how B2B sales people can get more leads. Most importantly, it delivers results! By following the steps Tom explained, I've already got high-quality leads worth £60,000 to £70,000 for cleaning contracts. All that came from implementing just a few of the tips Tom explained during the training session. If you're in sales, you need to book on one of Tom's courses as soon as possible! Given the cost of the courses, booking on one is a no-brainer! Without it, you're missing out on a goldmine of opportunities and large business contracts. Don't delay. Book a place today!"
– **Hana Smiddy**, Goldcrest Cleaning, Warwick

"At Rivo we deal with large global clients who want to manage safety, security and sustainability quickly and easily. So making contact with the right people in very large multi-national organisations is crucial. Tom's training was perfect to help us do this. A fantastic and informative session that I would highly recommend to other software sales teams."
– **Irfan Mamoojee**, global pre-sales director, Rivo Software, Warwick

"Tom's training course was a really valuable explanation of how to use B2B social media, particularly Linkedin, to get more in-bound leads. One of the big challenges we face is getting past gatekeepers and making contact with the right people in large multi-national organisations. Tom's training was invaluable in helping learn new ways to do this. I've had a Linkedin account for quite a while but learnt plenty of new stuff that I'm looking forward to putting into practice. Definitely worth your time if you're in sales!"
– **James Alexander Sinikson**, sales executive, Rivo Software, Warwick

"After setting up my own company, I came to Tom to find out exactly how I could use Linkedin to generate leads and business opportunities. I specialise in helping SMEs become more profitable and achieve their business objectives more easily through proper management of their finances. Tom's training was perfect. It showed me exactly how I could use Linkedin to get more business plus loads of valuable sales and marketing tips, strategies and techniques too. Definitely worth booking on one of Tom's courses ASAP." – **Chris Wright**, financial consultant

"As an owner of a Health & Safety Consultancy I was looking at how I could improve my understanding of LinkedIn and how it could be used to create more leads. I had met Tom at an event and expressed an interest in his training. I was not disappointed. Tom's training was invaluable. I didn't realise there were so many ways to use Linkedin to find potential customers and then get in touch quickly and easily. A jargon free, easy to understand session that I would recommend to anyone wanting to create potential leads." – **Jag Baines**, health and safety consultant

"I've had a Linkedin account for a long time but never quite understood how it could actually help to generate leads or win me more business – especially as I like to do business face-to-face. Tom's training was packed full of practical advice and information that mean I now know exactly how I can use Linkedin as part of my marketing and get more in-bound leads and warm phone calls. Highly recommended. Thanks Tom!"
– **Joanne Warren**, business consultant, Sunrise Business Support, Warwickshire

"I've had a Linkedin account for a long time but never quite understood how it could actually help to generate leads or win me more business – especially as I like to do business face-to-face. Tom's training was packed full of practical advice and information that mean I now know exactly how I can use Linkedin as part of my marketing and get more in-bound leads and

warm phone calls. Highly recommended. Thanks Tom!"
– **Jo Ciriani**, online marketer Jo's Correctional Facility, Warwickshire

"Tom has a deep understanding and knowledge of LinkedIn and its
potential attributes, not only as a connecting professional tool, but in its
potential for generating future sales leads. In a very short period of time he
managed to create many "ah-has" on how to effectively use LinkedIn as a
good sales tool. His approach is very personable , always willing to listen
and understand what is the need and the right path to address this fast and
efficiently. I would highly recommend Tom to anyone that needs to grow his
business and use available online tools (Twitter as well) to drive and create
more opportunities for his business."
– **Vasilis Karamalegos**, EMEA programme manager, Procter & Gamble

"I always thought I could use LinkedIn, until Tom showed more ways to
benefit from it and the features available. I highly recommend Tom, his
services and his knowledge to anyone or any business who are looking to
make the most from their LinkedIn experience."
– **Carl D. Pickering**, chief technology officer, Hedgehog Security

"Like many people I had a Linkedin profile but never really knew how to
utilise the tools & features available to me, that was until I attended one of
Tom's courses. Tom explained various methods of how to use LinkedIn to its
full potential. For anyone looking for new ways to expand their business I
would fully recommend one of Tom's courses."
– **Blaine Goldstraw**, business sales manager, M-Viron

"Tom provides excellent training on the use of LinkedIn. His understanding
of Linkedin is excellent and he explains very simply the steps required to
make full use of its capability. I would recommend Tom to anyone wanting
to generate warm sales leads!" – **Jack Pokoj**, energy consultant, Auditel

"Tom has a profound knowledge in branding and marketing. This, in
combination with his state-of-the-art knowledge and expertise of social
media, creates a very compelling value. I would recommend Tom to any
entrepreneur, businesses owner, or a person who is in a career transition
and, despite limited marketing budget, still needs to get more visibility in
the virtual market. Highly recommended!"
– **Dariusz Dzuiba**, global process manager, Hilti

"Tom was absolutely brilliant. Using the wording advised by Tom, I quickly made contact with a prospect and as a direct result of that meeting now have regular work. I wholeheartedly recommend Tom's LinkedIn training. It really does generate more business and it did for me."
– **Joan Goodger**, food safety trainer

"Initially I was not sure what I would learn from the training, as I had used LinkedIn for a little while. However, I was amazed by the amount that I did not know about LinkedIn and how much Tom taught me. I would highly recommend the LinkedIn training - very impressed!"
– **Emma Candlin**, JHPS Ltd, Staffordshire

"Tom's social media and LinkedIn training is well worth attending. I am now really well equipped to build my network of contacts on LinkedIn and ultimately connect with potential clients. I would not hesitate to recommend Tom's course and I am really looking forward to his follow up event." – **Julie Mrowicki-Green**, business psychologist, Purple Tulip

"I can highly recommend Tom for his LinkedIn training course which I have just attended. I learned many new tips including the need to be manage my contacts and groups and make them work better for me. I am hoping to raise my profile within the legal and mediation profession by following what I learned and would highly recommend Tom's course to other legal professionals."
– **Celia Christie**, family dispute resolution expert, Positive Family Mediation

"I recently attended an afternoon-long Linkedin training course run by Tom, and found it very helpful. Tom offers straight forward, easy to implement advice for making Linkedin a useful and productive business tool, and presents it in a clear and concise manner that makes it seem like common sense." – **Hazel Normandale**, Ant Hire, Leeds

"Tom's workshop was a great introduction to the new world of social selling and how it will help me develop business opportunities for Jigsaw CCS. We specialise in the fulfilment and delivery of creative direct mail marketing campaigns and as Business Development Manager for the company the more I can learn about other marketing channels the better. Tom's workshop was packed with great ideas, hints and tips, not just on LinkedIn but on marketing and business development in general. His training is ideal for anyone in marketing or business development who is not getting leads

from LinkedIn at the moment and wants to start! Good stuff Tom!"
– **Audrey Spriggs**, business development manager, Jigsaw CCS

"I attended a LinkedIn workshop that was run by Tom, I found it to be very useful and definitely worth the money. I have gained a lot of skills and knowledge from the workshop which I have taken away with me and put into practice within my workplace."
– **Emma McGranaghan**, Formation Media

"As someone new to LinkedIn, Tom's guidance and support has helped me take that first step - which is always the hardest. He is knowledgeable and has a friendly and approachable style. The take away guide and post training-day telephone support is particularly useful in overcoming the 'knowing-doing gap' of learning anything new."
– **Carole Thomson**, HR consultant, Warwickshire

"Tom delivered a great training session on LinkedIn and I came away with some key concepts that will aid the growth of my business."
– **David Wilson**, multi-level-marketing specialist, AdvertAnywhere

"Tom's course on Linked In was fantastic. He managed to make something I found very confusing into something very simple. I am now a lot more confident in developing my profile and believe it will come to great use in the future. It will be of great benefit here at Jigsaw CCS and I would recommend it for any other marketing companies looking for ways to connect with new business."
– **Charlotte Thompson**, business development executive, Jigsaw Complete Communications Services

"Tom's LinkedIn training session was, as I expected, full of useful tips, tricks and insights into getting more from the platform, but for me the most important and perhaps less expected aspect was how it was consistently structured around the simple but powerful message of using your profile as a proactive tool to create worthwhile connections and win more business. Added to that, Tom's confident and relaxed style kept the session flowing and maintained interest throughout. Highly recommended & definitely value for money!" – **Phil Buckley**, Enduring Solutions

"I have just attended Tom's LinkedIn Workshop and found it to be very helpful and informative. Tom's style is relaxed but knowledgeable and he fully addressed the needs of the participants over the three hours the workshop lasted. I have no hesitation in recommending this workshop for those who need to understand the benefits LinkedIn, as well as identify ways in which the platform can help you pro-actively market your business or services online." – **Tony Probert**, LightMedia Digital

"I found the session really informative and now understand much more clearly what Linkedin can bring to our business in terms of lead generation and client recommendations. Within a few hours I have improved my profile and have started to increase my connections. I would definitely recommend this course if you want to make more of Linkedin to generate business. Thank you Tom!" – **Liz Shuttleworth**, Hastam

"Tom is a natural coach. His knowledge of how to make the most of social media - and particularly Linkedin - is rooted in an understanding of what it means in a business environment, how it can contribute to personal and professional growth, and how to generate new business leads. He delivers this knowledge in a likeable, compelling and highly practical style. I thought I knew Linkedin. I now know that I'd only scratched the surface of its full potential as a business tool. His advice and expertise far outstripped my expectations and I'd highly recommend his services."
– **Nick Henderson**, Friday's PR

"Tom's advice and tips on Linkedin and its capabilities was an extremely useful exercise. I would thoroughly recommend him to other professionals who are trying to maximise the benefits of social media."
– **Edward Browne**, Robert Walters

"Tom has been extremely helpful in improving my understanding of how to use LinkedIn effectively. He knows what he is talking about and is very personable and generous with his advice as well as candid with his feedback. There is so much to learn about how to use LinkedIn to build relationships and to grow your business, that Tom's coaching has been very valuable. I would completely recommend his LinkedIn phone training to others." – **Monica Garcia-Romero**, Global Executive Coach

"I recently attended one of Tom's LinkedIn workshops and found it to be really helpful as well as enjoyable! Tom is hugely knowledgeable about the subject and I now feel that I have a much better understanding of how I can use LinkedIn to grow my own virtual assistant business. I would definitely recommend Tom's workshop to anyone who is looking to connect with like-

minded business people."
– **Denise Watson**, DW Business Support Services

"We attended one of Tom's courses for Linked-In. Tom is very passionate about Linked-In's ability to generate worthwhile business relationships and explained a number of very useful strategies and tips which we are about to embark upon. He also offered ongoing support. We have already recommended Tom to our colleagues in the group."
– **David Barnes**, Marshall Motor Group

"I would recommend Tom's Linked-In for Business seminar to anyone who, like me, did not previously truly appreciate or benefit from effective networking through social media. Simple to understand, this interactive workshop provided clear goals to work towards, and demonstrated tangible outcomes that enhance business success. A valuable session which has created a real desire, and ability, to engage with Linked-In, rather than just manage it." – **Kerry Draper**, HR consultant

"I attended one of Tom's Linked In courses last week and I am very glad I did! The most useful aspect for me was learning how Tom has implemented the tools and benefits of Linked In in his own business. His knowledge is wide, imaginative and well-honed. I now have a much better understanding of how I can use this valuable tool to market my own business and build relationships with potential referral partners. I would highly recommend that anyone that has simply dabbled with Linked In up until now gets themselves on one of Tom's courses so they can benefit in the same way I have. Thanks Tom - a very enjoyable and worthwhile course."
– **Sue Hearn**, Zenith Cost Consultancy

"Having just written-up my notes from Tom's "Helping you get more leads from Linkedin on 3 easy Steps" course, I now more fully appreciate just how much Tom taught me. The mind-map is BIG! The 3 key steps that he proposed make it simple for me to 'get going' ENJOYING social media. Use his course to find out how to ENJOY doing business using Linkedin as opposed to just doing business on Linkedin."
– **Greg Neumann**, Apple Mac IT consultant

"Sitting in on the end of one of Tom's workshops (to take some photographs), it was obvious that the delegates all had that same "lightbulb" moment saying I've been on LinkedIn for years but I've only just realised how I should have been using it. They clearly got a lot from his

training and were going away heads buzzing full of ideas and with plans to put what they had learned into action."
– **David Morphew**, photographer

"I attended Tom's Linkedin training course on May 9th. I would highly recommend this course to anyone who is looking to use Linkedin to generate more leads and to identify potential clients, as well as the best ways to contact them. I left this course with some great tips on how to strengthen my profile and how I can get the most out of Linkedin for my business."
– **Andrew Dix**, financial advisor, Future Perfect Financial Solutions

"I have just attended Tom's workshop on 'Getting more leads from Linkedin'. This was a great session giving helpful insight in how to make the most of my profile on Linkedin and how to connect with potential clients and contacts. I am looking forward to putting the tools and techniques into practice to increase my network on Linkedin. I would definitely recommend this session to people who want to learn more. It is brilliant value for money also. Thank you Tom!"
– **Tracey Parkinson**, health and safety marketing executive, Hastam

"I attended Tom's course 3 easy steps and even as an existing Linkedin user, I learnt useful new information. I now feel better able to use Linkedin to find new leads and I Would recommend the course to other people who want to find new customers more easily. It was time usefully spent and I know as long as I put into action what Tom showed I will get results."
– **Taruna Chauhan**, healthcare sector business consultant

"I met with Tom to learn more about LinkedIn and how to improve my profile in preparation for launching my new business. Tom presented his steps for getting known, building relationships and turning cold leads into warm ones. The training has already enabled me to not only update my profile but - more importantly - establish a clear plan of action to improve visibility, generate good content and gain credibility in the industry. I'm sure this will be invaluable as I prepare to launch and in developing sales later. Thanks Tom!" – **Gill Searl**, owner, Linguagloss

"Tom delivered a clear and informative overview of what LinkedIn was and what it is capable of achieving. I learnt that it could be a very useful tool for sales and marketing. I would think that other sales/marketing professionals

would benefit from this type of workshop."
– **Shuk Quan Somani**, business development coordinator, Ant Hire

"Excellent at social media and development."
– **Oliver Roberts**, sales and marketing, JustQuoteMe Ltd

"Great tips and lots to think about. I recommend anyone looking to learn how to use Linkedin enrolls on one of Tom's workshops."
– **June Irani**, health and wellbeing specialist

"Tom's Linkedin taster session was a great introduction and overview of this fantastic tool and left me keen to learn more. In the short timespan I now feel able to use most of the features of LinkedIn for my business and would recommend anyone in B2B to take this training – it's clear immediately the results it can bring to your business."
– **Rachel Mousell**, owner and founder, The Marketing Tree

"Tom has the skills, abilities and knowledge required to be a great social media trainer. I had the opportunity to receive his advice and since then my understanding of LinkedIn has just increased."
– **Andres Sanchez Sandaza**

"I found workshop run by Tom exceeded my expectations as it opened up areas of LinkedIn I hadn't yet explored. Even from my first telephone conversation with Tom the week previously, he was suggesting snappy headline improvements to my profile which has already seen an increase of new connections by over a quarter. I'm looking forward to uploading many pieces of imported information currently held as a PDF and on YouTube. I would recommend his workshop to others."
– **Adam Holland**, network marketing specialist, Forever Living Products

"After attending Tom's Linkedin workshop I had a thorough understanding of how I could use the platform effectively. The training was useful because it was delivered in a practical and tangible format.   I now feel much more confident about using Linkedin as a networking tool and feel I have the know-how to build the right connections to grow my business, it's now just over to me to implement a strategy. I would definitely recommend this workshop." – **Rose Meredith** (nee Lord), Image Consultant

"Having known Tom as a social media expert, I reached out to him as I needed some help to improve my LinkedIn profile. Tom quickly understood

my needs and provided me with tips and walked me through with a simple yet effective video, tailored to suit my needs. Although I consider myself very proficient, Tom was still able to add value to my profile and now, I know more features of LinkedIn. I think this ability to understand the needs of the customer, work with you closely and quickly bring in value-add makes Tom, a well rounded strategist. With no second thoughts, I would refer anyone who needs any social media help to Tom."
– **Ramkumar Viswanathan**, business improvement manager, Telefonica UK

"Tom is very knowledgeable about social media and in particular Linkedin optimisation. I've found Tom to be very helpful and would recommend his consultation services."
– **Errol Lawson**, professional speaker, author and pastor

"I would definitely recommend Tom to other business people."
– **Gianluca Del Frate**, subsea project engineer, Wood Group Kenny Ltd

"Tom's social media training was fantastic and exceeded by my expectations of what was possible through Linkedin. I definitely feel better equipped to use social media as a business tool and for finding new career opportunities. I would definitely recommend him to others!"
– **Clare Chan**, Business Consultant, Logistics Consulting Asia

"Tom went way beyond the usual boundaries of helping me."
– **Ernie Boxall**, personal trainer and shiatsu therapist

"Tom showed me how to use Linkedin properly, rather than just collecting connections. His training is engaging and useful with clear B2B benefits."
– **Neil Kennett**, managing director, Featurebank Ltd

"Tom really knows what he's talking about. The tips I received from Tom helped transform my profile and I can't wait to spread the word! Thanks again Tom."
– **Alexandra Stuart-Hutcheson**, Business Development Manager, Accordance

To find out how you could get more leads from Linkedin more easily and more often in 3 easy steps, simply call Tom Mallens at Social Innovation Media Ltd on +44 (0)1926 678 920, email tom@tommallens.com or tweet @TomMallens.

A SECRET THAT MIGHT SHOCK YOU

I'd like to tell you a secret. One that transformed how I think about marketing.

And skyrocketed the results I got in business.

I learnt it from an interesting man called Stefan, who I bumped into at an otherwise pretty forgettable and grey networking event.

It was the secret of writing more persuasively.

So that anyone reading what you write is more likely to read it all. And then, actually do what you ask at the end.

If you can write words that sell effectively, and speak persuasively in front of people too, then you've got a winning combination.

And you tend to sell a lot more in process.

If you sign-up for my emails at
www.tommallens.com/moreleadsfromlinkedin
then you'll learn how to write words that do your selling for you.

And loads of other invaluable stuff too.

Which means you'll make your job easier and get better results as well.

It's free. And it only takes 30 seconds.

Just go to www.tommallens.com/moreleadsfromlinkedin now.

Lightning Source UK Ltd.
Milton Keynes UK
UKOW06f0134050615

252943UK00002B/45/P